THE LAYMAN'S BIBLE COMMENTARY
IN TWENTY-FIVE VOLUMES

THE LAYMAN'S BIBLE COMMENT

THE LAYMAN'S
BIBLE COMMENTARY

Balmer H. Kelly, *Editor*

Donald G. Miller   *Associate Editors*   Arnold B. Rhodes

Dwight M. Chalmers, *Editor, John Knox Press*

VOLUME 22

THE LETTER OF PAUL TO THE

GALATIANS

THE LETTER OF PAUL TO THE

EPHESIANS

THE LETTER OF PAUL TO THE

PHILIPPIANS

THE LETTER OF PAUL TO THE

COLOSSIANS

Archibald M. Hunter

JOHN KNOX PRESS

ATLANTA, GEORGIA

Published in Great Britain by SCM Press Ltd., London.

Tenth printing 1977

Complete set: ISBN: 0-8042-0326-9
This volume: 0-8042-3022-6
Library of Congress Card Number: 59-10454
Printed in the United States of America

PREFACE

The LAYMAN'S BIBLE COMMENTARY is based on the conviction that the Bible has the Word of good news for the whole world. The Bible is not the property of a special group. It is not even the property and concern of the Church alone. It is given to the Church for its own life but also to bring God's offer of life to all mankind—wherever there are ears to hear and hearts to respond.

It is this point of view which binds the separate parts of the LAYMAN'S BIBLE COMMENTARY into a unity. There are many volumes and many writers, coming from varied backgrounds, as is the case with the Bible itself. But also as with the Bible there is a unity of purpose and of faith. The purpose is to clarify the situations and language of the Bible that it may be more and more fully understood. The faith is that in the Bible there is essentially one Word, one message of salvation, one gospel.

The LAYMAN'S BIBLE COMMENTARY is designed to be a concise, non-technical guide for the layman in personal study of his own Bible. Therefore, no biblical text is printed along with the comment upon it. This commentary will have done its work precisely to the degree in which it moves its readers to take up the Bible for themselves.

The writers have used the Revised Standard Version of the Bible as their basic text. Occasionally they have differed from this translation. Where this is the case they have given their reasons. In the main, no attempt has been made either to justify the wording of the Revised Standard Version or to compare it with other translations.

The objective in this commentary is to provide the most helpful explanation of fundamental matters in simple, up-to-date terms. Exhaustive treatment of subjects has not been undertaken.

In our age knowledge of the Bible is perilously low. At the same time there are signs that many people are longing for help in getting such knowledge. Knowledge of and about the Bible is, of course, not enough. The grace of God and the work of the Holy Spirit are essential to the renewal of life through the Scriptures. It is in the happy confidence that the great hunger for the Word is a sign of God's grace already operating within men, and that the Spirit works most wonderfully where the Word is familiarly known, that this commentary has been written and published.

THE EDITORS AND
THE PUBLISHERS

THE LETTER OF PAUL TO THE

GALATIANS

INTRODUCTION

"The Letter to the Galatians"—how formal, sedate, and impassive is the title of this letter that blazes with passion and must have come red-hot out of the writer's heart! It is not a treatise but a sword-cut in a battle, dealt, in an hour of great peril, by a combatant facing formidable foes. No wonder Martin Luther loved this letter, declaring himself "betrothed" to it. Like Paul, Luther was a liberator and knew that great issues were at stake; and when you pierce beneath the historical accidents to the spiritual essentials, you discover that the two men were fighting much the same battle—a battle for the very truth of the gospel, a battle for spiritual liberty. So, from Paul's day to this, the Letter to the Galatians has been the "Charter of Christian Freedom"—freedom not only from the Law of Moses, but from every yoke imposed on the religious life as an external condition of salvation. Its message, summarily stated, is: "For freedom Christ has set us free; stand fast therefore, and do not submit again to a yoke of slavery" (5:1).

Nobody in his senses has ever doubted that Paul wrote this letter. The style is the man, and every paragraph bears his marks, speaks his accents. As well doubt that Carlyle wrote *Sartor Resartus* or Walt Whitman, *Leaves of Grass*! There is not, however, complete agreement by all interpreters concerning two points: who Paul's readers were, and when he wrote the letter. These two questions will be discussed first.

The Readers

Who were the "foolish Galatians"? (3:1).

The old view, championed by Bishop Lightfoot and still held by many Continental scholars, is that Paul uses the word "Galatia" in its *geographical* sense. He is writing to Christians in such towns as Ancyra (modern Angora or Ankara, the capital of Turkey), and Pessinus, situated in the ancient kingdom of Galatia—a wild country where "Gauls" had settled in the third century B.C.

Paul is said to have visited this region on his second and third missionary journeys (Acts 16:6; 18:23). This is called the North Galatian view.

The new view, championed by Sir William Ramsay and most British and American scholars, holds that Paul uses "Galatia" in its *political* sense. Galatia, in this view, means the Roman province formed in 25 B.C., which included, besides the ancient kingdom, parts of Lycaonia, Pisidia, and Phrygia. In this province lay the churches of South Galatia—Antioch, Derbe, Lystra, and Iconium—founded during Paul's first journey (Acts 13 and 14). It was his converts in this region whom he addressed in his letter. This is the South Galatian view.

Which view is right?

When did Paul visit the ancient kingdom of Galatia? The "North Galatianists" point in evidence to Acts 16:6 and 18:23: "They [Paul and Timothy] went through the region of Phrygia and Galatia" (Acts 16:6). "[Paul] went from place to place through the region of Galatia and Phrygia" (Acts 18:23). The "South Galatianists" reply that this is not evidence, for the words refer to that part of Phrygia which had been taken into the Roman province of Galatia.

The "North Galatianists" then adduce further arguments:

1. In Acts, Luke does not call Antioch, Lystra, Derbe, and Iconium towns of Galatia. Therefore it is improbable that Paul would have done so.

2. Pisidia, Phrygia, and Lycaonia are treated as geographical terms in Acts. Galatia in Paul's letter must be the same.

3. The fickleness of the Galatians (Gal. 1:6) agrees very well with their Gallic origin. (As if any nation had a monopoly on this failing!)

In reply the "South Galatianists" marshal arguments like these:

1. Paul, the Roman citizen, elsewhere in his letters thinks in terms of Roman provinces (Achaia, Macedonia, and the like). Therefore he does so in Galatians.

2. North Galatia—a wild country with poor communications —was hardly open enough for Paul's enemies, the Judaizers, to have dogged his footsteps there. (Conceivably, however, the Judaizers were local people.)

3. Paul assumes that Barnabas was well known to his readers (Gal. 2:1, 13), as indeed he was to the cities of South Galatia, having visited them in Paul's company.

4. Galatians 4:14 possibly refers to the incident at Lystra described in Acts 14:12.

5. There is no unambiguous evidence that Paul ever was in the ancient kingdom of Galatia.

How shall we conclude? The case for North Galatia is arguable; but the evidence for South Galatia is more impressive and is convincing.

The Date

In the North Galatian view, the Letter to the Galatians was written after the visit of Acts 18:23, during Paul's third missionary journey, possibly from Ephesus about A.D. 55.

In the South Galatian view, it may have been written either before or after the Apostolic Council of A.D. 49 (Acts 15). Those who put it after, point to the theological similarities between Galatians and the letters written during Paul's third journey (I and II Corinthians and Romans) as proof that it must have been written about the same time, say A.D. 55.

But the strong argument for putting it before the Apostolic Council is the letter's complete silence about the apostolic decree described in Acts 15. That decree settled the point at issue in Galatia, with the decision that Gentile converts need not be circumcised. If Paul had been writing after the Council, he would surely have quoted the decree and closed the issue.

If this is the truth, then Galatians is the earliest of Paul's letters and was written about A.D. 49, either at Antioch or on the way up to Jerusalem.

The Occasion of the Letter

The occasion which gave rise to this letter is not in doubt. Since Paul had left Galatia, certain "Judaizers" (Jewish Christians zealous to preserve Jewish customs and to graft the gospel on to the Law of Moses) had appeared there, and were persuading Paul's converts that circumcision and observance of the Law were essential to a true Christianity. This flatly contradicted Paul's gospel of the grace of God; so the Judaizers were at pains to vilify Paul's credentials by saying that he was a compromiser or, at best, a secondhand apostle who had learned everything from Peter and James, the "pillar apostles." Paul wrote at once, in great passion of spirit, to counteract this Judaizing propaganda, to assert his complete apostolic independence, and to explain the deepest principles of the gospel.

The Message of Galatians

The problem handled in Galatians is this: What makes a man a Christian? Is it circumcision and keeping the Law, or faith in Christ? Paul's answer is in Galatians 5:6: "External things like circumcision," he says in effect, "do not matter. What matters is faith in Christ, working through love."

Paul and the Judaizers alike in some sense believed in Christ. The question at issue was whether for *perfect* Christianity anything else was needed. The Judaizers said, Yes. The Gentile faith in Christ was all very well for a start, but it was not enough. If these "foreign believers" (the Gentiles) were to be really good Christians, and inherit salvation along with the Jews (had not Jesus himself said that "salvation is of the Jews"?), their simple faith in Christ would have to be supplemented by circumcision and the observance of the Law of Moses. Just as emphatically Paul said, No. Christ, he said, is the whole of Christianity, Christ crucified and risen. He is God's gift of grace to man's faith, and all that sinful man must do is to respond to that gift with trust and obedience. Christ has died for our sins; and when a sinful man puts his complete trust in Christ, God accepts him, forgives him, sets his feet on the road to salvation, and gives him the Holy Spirit to enable him to lead the new life. This was the heart of the gospel. Paul did not dispute the Christian standing of those who clung to older forms; but he was quite adamant that they were not necessary for salvation, and that to regard them as indispensable (as the Judaizers did) was to pervert the gospel of God's grace.

Yes, the modern reader may say, but circumcision and keeping the Law of Moses are no longer issues which face us today. Must not this letter, therefore, have lost all its relevance for the modern man?

The answer is emphatically in the negative. The issue Paul discusses in this letter always keeps cropping up in Christian history. It cropped up for Martin Luther before the Reformation. It still keeps arising in new forms; for it is part of the bigger question, the ultimate question for religion: How is a sinful man to get right with God? Is it by keeping the Law—in modern terms, by keeping the Ten Commandments and living as Christ tells us in the Sermon on the Mount? No; these things we *ought* to do, but we *cannot*. What man alive, for example, will dare to claim that he lives his life according to the sublime precepts of the great Sermon? The truth is that no man can, by his own exertions, put himself right with God. Let mortal man present himself before the holy God clad in all his good works (as the Pharisee in the parable tried to present himself) and the divine verdict on him must always be, "Unrighteous!" There is no such thing as a religiously "self-made" man. We cannot save ourselves. The way to acceptance with God is not by works (as the Judaizers thought and as a great many people have thought since), but by faith in God's Christ who has died and risen to save us from our sins. And real goodness—Christian goodness—is the *result*, not the prerequisite, of our faith. The Judaizers said: "Do these things, and live." The Christian says: "Live, and do these things." Thus the Christian life, which Paul describes in the last two chapters, is not some punctilious observance of a mass of rules and regulations, but the living of the good life with the aid of Christ's example and teaching and with the help of the Holy Spirit.

Thus, though circumcision and the observance of the Law are no longer live issues, the Letter to the Galatians remains relevant to our need. Whenever any religious rite is made co-ordinate with faith in Christ as the condition of salvation, this letter becomes a sword of the Spirit to strike the error down. Salvation is by faith in Christ alone. Small wonder that Galatians has been called "the Epistle of Christian Freedom" and "the Magna Charta of Evangelical Christianity."

OUTLINE

The Letter to the Galatians can be roughly divided into three
sections. The first, which is autobiographical, covers the first two
chapters. In it Paul vindicates his apostolic independence in face
of the attacks made upon him. The second, which is doctrinal,
takes in chapters 3 and 4. In it Paul sets the choice before the
Galatians—Christ or the Law?—and argues for its urgency. In
the last two chapters, which are ethical and practical, he bids
them walk in the Spirit and warns them against abusing their
Christian freedom. The letter ends with a postscript in Paul's
own "large letters."

The following analysis of contents is that found in the commentary:

Address. Galatians 1:1-5

The Personal Question. Galatians 1:6—2:21

    The Reason for Writing (1:6-10)
    Conversion and Call (1:11-17)
    The First Visit to Jerusalem (1:18-24)
    The Second Visit to Jerusalem (2:1-10)
    The Clash Between Paul and Peter at Antioch (2:11-21)

The Doctrinal Argument. Galatians 3:1—4:31

    The Appeal to Experience (3:1-5)
    The Faith of Abraham (3:6-9)
    The Curse of the Law (3:10-14)
    The Law's Purpose (3:15-22)
    The Law Our Custodian (3:23-29)
    Freedom as Sons (4:1-7)
    Warning Against Relapse (4:8-11)
    A Personal Appeal (4:12-20)
    The Allegory of Sarah and Hagar (4:21-31)

The Practical Application. Galatians 5:1—6:10

    Choose Freedom (5:1-12)
    Not License but Love, Not Flesh but Spirit (5:13-26)
    Sundry Christian Counsels (6:1-10)

Autograph Postscript. Galatians 6:11-18

COMMENTARY

ADDRESS

Galatians 1:1-5

"A to B, greeting," with an added prayer for the health of the reader, was the usual way an ancient letter began. Paul likes to expand this conventional beginning, either by stressing his own credentials (as here), or by summarizing his gospel (as in the Letter to the Romans).

Paul opens with a vigorous assertion that his apostleship is of direct divine origin. To say that he is an Apostle, that is, the "special messenger" of Christ, is not enough; he must underline the authenticity of his apostleship, since his enemies are impugning it. The sentence between dashes, therefore, says in effect, "If I am an apostle, as I surely am, it is because God through Christ, and not any man or group of men, made me one." He adds the words "who raised him from the dead" because it was the risen Christ who had commissioned him as an Apostle. With himself he associates all the brethren who were with him, possibly referring to Christian friends going up with him from Antioch to Jerusalem. His addressees are the churches in Galatia; in other words, the Christian communities in Derbe, Lystra, Iconium, and (Pisidian) Antioch in the Roman province of Galatia.

At this point (1:3) a pagan correspondent was usually contented to use a Greek word which conveyed a simple greeting. Paul Christianizes the greeting by using a word of similar sound meaning "grace," God's wonderful kindness to undeserving men shown in the gift of Christ. With it he links the usual oriental greeting of "peace," though no doubt he thinks of it primarily in the sense of peace *with God*, or reconciliation. Grace and peace come from "God the Father and our Lord Jesus Christ." God and Christ are associated in a divine unity, God being called by the name which Christ had taught his disciples to use—"Father."

The title, "Lord," conferred on Jesus after his exaltation (Acts 2:36; Phil. 2:9), set him forth as a being worthy of worship. "Jesus is Lord" was probably the earliest Christian creed. But for Paul, Christ is not properly described without a reference to the Cross: "who gave himself for our sins" (1:4). Here the fact of the Atonement is stated simply in words that are reminiscent of the Lord's saying that he had come "to give his life as a ransom for many" (Mark 10:45). However hard we may find it to make a satisfactory theory about the Atonement, the belief that Christ "gave himself for our sins" is a cardinal Christian doctrine. The purpose of the Atonement was "to deliver us from the present evil age." By his death, Paul says, Jesus has delivered us from the present evil age (the order of time), which like "the world" (the order of space), lies, as John says, in the power of the Devil (I John 5:19). This death is declared by Paul to be "according to the will of our God and Father." God willed it, not merely permitted it; it was more than a martyr's death, it was a Redeemer's. The thought of our great redemption moves Paul to close his salutation with a doxology (1:5).

THE PERSONAL QUESTION
Galatians 1:6—2:21

The Reason for Writing (1:6-10)

Following such a salutation, Paul normally would have moved into a thanksgiving for his readers' Christian progress. But as he considers the situation in Galatia, he can find no cause for giving thanks; instead of progress the news is of retrogression. So, without any finesse, he plunges into the central theme of his letter: to rest salvation on anything but the sheer grace of God is to replace the gospel by something which is a complete perversion of it.

"I am astonished that you are so quickly deserting him [God the Father] who called you in the grace of Christ" (1:6). "So quickly" means so soon after their conversion. How brief had been their loyalty! Paul, in preaching to the Galatians, had dwelt on God's sheer grace in calling men into his Kingdom. Under the influence of the Judaizers, however, his converts were now turning to a different gospel—not that there was another gospel, but there were some who were troubling them and wanting to pervert the gospel of Christ. First, Paul apparently says (the Greek has two words for "another" here, making the precise meaning difficult) that "some who trouble you," that is, the Judaizers, are proclaiming a different gospel. Then he corrects himself: "You really cannot call it a different gospel—there is only one—and what these Judaizers are preaching is a perversion of it. They want to adulterate the gospel of God's grace with legalism." In plain terms, what the Judaizers were saying was this: "To be a Christian, you must not only believe in Christ, you must also accept circumcision and keep the Law of Moses." Indignantly, Paul pronounces a curse on all who corrupt the gospel (1:8-9). "As we have said before" must refer to some previous warning Paul had given them, probably by word of mouth. "Accursed" is the Greek word "anathema." This in turn represents a Hebrew word which means something "devoted" to God, usually for destruction (for example, Jericho in Joshua 6:17-21) and, therefore, "accursed."

It is clear, from verse 10, that the Judaizers had insinuated that Paul was some kind of compromiser, trying to make converts by any means. Probably they said something like this: "Paul is trying to please men by abolishing the Law and so getting rid of an essential part of the gospel." Now we know—for he has told us so himself, for example in I Corinthians 9:19-23, with which compare Acts 21:17-26—that Paul did go out of his way to "conciliate" men when no vital issue was at stake. Where, however, the very truth of the gospel was at issue, he was as firm as adamant, as he is in this particular passage. "Read what I have just said," he says in effect, "and tell me if these are the accents of a compromiser." He goes on to say, "If I were still pleasing men, I should not be a servant of Christ." The principle stated here is Christ's own: "No man can serve two masters." "If popularity with men were all I am concerned about, I could think of many easier ways of achieving it than choosing the career of a Christian missionary." It is as if somebody today were to charge Albert Schweitzer with seeking the limelight by his mission work in the swamps of Lambarene!

Conversion and Call (1:11-17)

Here begins an autobiographical section proving Paul's independence, as an apostle, of any human authority.

Paul reiterates his claim to have received the gospel direct from Christ (1:11-12). He did not sit at the feet of any human teacher who indoctrinated him in its truth; rather it came to him, as in the German expression, "perpendicularly from on high"; he received it through a "revelation of Jesus Christ." He means that Jesus Christ was revealed to him in such a way that

he had now a gospel to preach. Of course, he is thinking of the
Damascus Road experience. What, then, did Paul receive on the
Damascus Road, apart from the realization that Jesus Christ was
alive? Was it a knowledge of the chief facts about the life and
teaching of Jesus? Probably not; these, in however garbled a
version, he must already have known as a persecutor. What he
got on the Damascus Road was a *true understanding* of these
facts. Jesus, he learned in that high hour, was not an impostor,
but God's Son.

Then Paul gives us a "flash back" into his past life (1:13-14).
Why? To show that nothing in his previous career predisposed
him toward the gospel. "Why," he says in effect, "when this
wonderful thing happened to me, I was known as the most rabid
of Jewish traditionalists. How furiously I persecuted the Church
and harried it!" (The reader will find other references to Paul's
past life in I Corinthians 15:8-10; Philippians 3:5-6; I Timothy
1:13; Acts 22:3-5; 26:4-5.) Paul was, of course, "a Pharisee of
the Pharisees"; he belonged to the strictest sect of "practicing
Jews." More than that, while some of his young Jewish contemporaries were content to sit rather loosely to the faith of their
fathers—they have their counterparts today in Christianity!—he
was notorious as a fanatical defender of the ancestral religion.

Then came the sheer miracle of his conversion (1:15-16).
(Other allusions to his conversion will be found in I Corinthians
9:1; 15:5-8; II Corinthians 4:6; Philippians 3:12.) Let the
reader mark carefully the phrases Paul uses to describe it. Every
one of them is deliberately chosen to stress the divine initiative
in all that happened—"set apart," "called," "through his grace,"
"was pleased to reveal." Paul's apostolate came from very far-off
Sources!

First, Paul traces the predestinating purpose of God in all that
befell him. "God," he says, "had set me apart before I was
born." The words remind us of the call of the Servant of the
Lord in Isaiah 49:1, as they are reminiscent also of the call of
Jeremiah in Jeremiah 1:5. The idea of election is of course basic
to Paul's theology, as it appears, for example, in Ephesians 1:4-5
and in Romans 8:29-30. In Christian history it has sometimes
been so perverted as to bring it into deserved disrepute. But the
doctrine is not absurd and untenable, as its mockers suppose. Is
it not basically the belief that we do not just *happen* to exist,
that our life has its roots in eternity, and that our salvation be-

gins in the mind of the eternal God (as the work of art begins in the mind of the artist)? What election means in simple terms is this: God chooses us before we choose him; God does not choose us because we deserve it; and God does not choose us to be his favorites but to be his servants. With all three of these propositions Paul would have heartily agreed.

Verse 16 tells how God's electing purpose for Paul found its fulfillment. God "was pleased to reveal his Son to me." The sentence almost suggests God's drawing back a corner of the curtain that hides the unseen world and disclosing to Paul his well-beloved Son. (A parallel may be found, perhaps, in the Transfiguration.) As everybody knows, the Book of Acts contains three accounts of Paul's conversion (chapters 9, 22, and 26). These stress the external phenomena accompanying the event, whereas Paul stresses here the *internal* experience. Perhaps II Corinthians 4:6 is the best commentary on this experience. What God did for Paul was to open his spiritual eyes so that he saw Christ in his true character, no longer as a hated impostor but as the very Son of the Highest.

God, as we have said, chooses men to be his servants, not his favorites. So it was with Paul. The revelation brought with it a commission—"that I might preach him among the Gentiles" (see also Acts 9:15). Note that the commission really grew out of his conversion; it was no afterthought. Is not this psychologically very likely? As a Jew, Paul must often have discussed the terms on which Gentiles might be admitted to Israel's privileges, and he no doubt took a rigorist line in the discussion. Then Stephen's teaching showed him that the new faith meant the abolition of the old privileges, and when he became a Christian, he knew at once that this meant accepting Jesus as the Savior of all men.

But this part of the letter is primarily concerned with what happened to Paul after the revelation and the commission. "I did not confer with flesh and blood," he says (1:16). His foes, the Judaizers, were saying (let us remember), that his authority stemmed from the original Apostles. "On the contrary," Paul replies, "after the revelation I consulted with no human being; instead of going up to Jerusalem to be briefed by the original Apostles, off I went at once to Arabia." Thus the Jerusalem Apostles had nothing to do with the central experience which gave Paul his apostolic commission. But where was "Arabia" and what was Paul doing there? Formerly students of a romantic turn of mind pictured Paul making his long way south to the Sinai Peninsula as Elijah had done (I Kings 19:8-18). But Arabia was a vast desert area which reached practically to the gates of Damascus itself. And since we know that the Arabs around Damascus were soon "thirsting for his blood"—witness II Corinthians 11:33 and compare Acts 9:25—we may fairly take Paul's "Arabia" to be the country of the Nabatean Arabs, east of Damascus. It is altogether likely that Paul was still trying to think out all the implications of his great experience, but it is also likely that at this time he was trying his prentice hand at Christian preaching, hence the hostility of the neighboring Arabs. (Who was it said that, wherever Paul went, he raised either a riot or a revival?)

Let us remark, finally, that Acts says nothing of the journey to Arabia. The two visits to Damascus implied in Paul's verb "returned" appear as one in Acts 9:19-25. This is one of several evidences that Luke, in writing Acts, did not have Paul's letters at his elbow.

The First Visit to Jerusalem (1:18-24)

Paul now describes his first visit to Jerusalem as a Christian. His point here is that, except for this one brief visit to see Peter, he had no contact for many years with the Church in Jerusalem. This is the visit recorded in Acts 9:26-30. It took place three years after his conversion. Now, if Paul was converted in A.D. 33, as many believe, three years later would be A.D. 35, since, on the Jewish system of inclusive reckoning, three years need mean no more than one year and bits of two others. The purpose of the visit was to "make the acquaintance" of Cephas (Peter's name in Aramaic); the verb Paul uses is commonly used of visiting an important personage with a view to making his acquaintance. Paul's meaning here is that he went up to Jerusalem to get to know Peter, *not* to get instruction from him. The only other notable he met during his fortnight's stay was James "the Lord's brother" (1:19). The phrase distinguishes him from James the son of Zebedee whom Herod put to death (Acts 12:2), but the Greek does not make it clear whether James ranked as an apostle. This James, not believing in his Brother during the days of his flesh, rose to belief in him after the Resurrection (I Cor. 15:7), and became the leader of the mother Church in Jerusalem. What, precisely, was his relationship to Jesus? The simple and natural answer is: a younger brother. Other theories which make him a stepbrother—that is, a son of Joseph by a previous marriage—or a cousin are not supported by evidence in Scripture.

Halfway through his paragraph Paul stops to confirm his statement with an oath: "Before God, I do not lie!" (1:20), because obviously his first contact with the Jerusalem Apostles was of decisive importance. What he means is this: "A brief visit of a fortnight, a meeting with only two of the Jerusalem authorities—this was the sum of it. I did not see the rest of the Apostles, and any suggestion that the Twelve commissioned me is patently absurd."

"Then I went into the regions of Syria and Cilicia" (1:21). Acts 9:26-30 tells us what made him leave Jerusalem—his bold preaching to the Hellenistic (Greek-speaking) Jews. When they threatened to kill him, the Jerusalem Christians smuggled Paul down to Caesarea on the coast and sent him to Tarsus in Cilicia, his native place. There, though we know nothing directly about it, he must have begun missionary work in earnest.

Paul's final comment on this visit (1:22-24) is that, though known in Jerusalem, he was at this time a complete stranger to the churches in Judea, that is, in the country districts outside Jerusalem. All they heard was: "Our former persecutor is now preaching the faith he once harried," and hearing it, they thanked God for it. "Faith" here means "religion," much as we talk today about "the Faith" (see also 3:23 and 6:10).

The Second Visit to Jerusalem (2:1-10)

Paul is still recording his early movements to show his independence of those who were his elders in the faith. Now, telling of his second visit to Jerusalem, he puts on record how the Jerusalem authorities recognized his mission, acknowledged his gospel as complete, and gave him their blessing.

This visit we take to be the same as that described in Acts 11:30, the so-called "famine visit." The alternative is to identify Galatians 2:1-10 with the Apostolic Council visit recorded in Acts 15. This we reject for two main reasons: first, Galatians 2:1-10 describes a private discussion, whereas Acts 15 describes a public meeting. Second, to accept this view is to imply that Paul deliberately ignored the visit described in Acts 11:30, thus making a grave omission at the very time he was determined to assert his complete truthfulness, as indicated by his words in 1:20: "In what I am writing to you, before God, I do not lie!"

"Then after fourteen years I went up again to Jerusalem with Barnabas, taking Titus along with me" (2:1). Notice first that according to the Jewish inclusive system of reckoning, "fourteen" need mean no more than "thirteen" (see discussion of 1:18). If Paul is again reckoning from his conversion (A.D. 33), as seems likely, this second visit occurred about A.D. 46. This date agrees roughly with what we know, from Jewish sources, about the famine in the reign of the Roman Emperor Claudius, to which Acts 11:28-30 alludes. Barnabas, be it noted, is assumed to be well known to the Galatians, a point in favor, incidentally, of the South Galatian theory. The manner of referring to Titus seems to imply that he held a subordinate position.

Why did Paul undertake this visit? He says that he "went up by revelation" (2:2). In Acts 11:28 the famine visit is described as the consequence of Agabus' prophecy. This is probably what Paul has in mind: "I went up to Jerusalem, not because I wished to get guidance from the elder Apostles, but because I knew, from Agabus' prediction, that God meant me to go." But though famine relief was the main object of the visit, Paul used the occasion to have a private discussion about his gospel with "those who were of repute"—"the people of consequence," we might paraphrase it. Possibly Paul's opponents had used the phrase. If so, it ought to be placed in quotation marks in the text. Verse 9 shows that the three chiefs were James, Peter, and John. Why did Paul submit his gospel to the people of consequence? The answer he gives is in the last clause of verse 2: "lest somehow I should be running or had run in vain." He was anxious to know that the Jerusalem Apostles approved his gospel as it concerned the Gentiles. If they had said that all Gentile converts must be circumcised, Paul's work would have been stultified.

So far, so good; but now in verses 3-5 the excitement of the controversy has torn the grammar to tatters, so that we cannot be sure what Paul means. The sentence is about Titus and circumcision and certain false brethren, but whether Paul is admitting that Titus was in fact circumcised (as a concession to the Judaizers), or whether he is saying the precise opposite—that is, that he declined to have Titus circumcised and that the leaders gave way in their demand—is anybody's guess. Both views have the support of good interpreters of the letter. Some take Paul to be saying: "Titus, who was a non-Jew, was indeed circumcised, but there was no question of compulsion—I allowed it as a concession." In proof they point to Acts 16:3. There Paul is found circumcising Timothy. But the parallel is not conclusive evidence, since Timothy's mother was a Jewess, whereas Titus was a pure Gentile. The majority of interpreters, finding it very hard to believe that Paul would have given way in this "test case," take the sentence to mean: "The Apostles did not *enforce* the circumcision of Titus, so that he remained uncircumcised." This is the view to which we incline, with much hesitation. What is clear is that some men were desperately keen to have Titus circumcised. These Paul calls "false brethren secretly brought in, who slipped in to spy out our freedom which we have in Christ Jesus, that they might bring us into bondage" (2:4). Who were these interlopers? Apparently they were militant legalists surreptitiously smuggled into the meeting. Paul calls them "spies," whose aim was not freedom but slavery. But he adds: "We were so determined that the freedom of the gospel should be preserved that we refused to make even a moment's compromise with them." (In verse 5 the Revised Standard Version follows the best manuscripts and includes the negative. One or two of the manuscripts, however, omit the word "not." If this were the true reading, the sense would be, "But because of false brethren we did make a brief concession." But if Paul, in this fashion, did give way, how could he possibly say that his aim was to preserve the truth of the gospel for Gentiles? Would he not in fact have been betraying it?)

The sense of the next verse (2:6) is clear, although the syntax is broken. Paul says, in effect: "The people of consequence— what their status used to be (namely, companions of Jesus during his earthly ministry) makes no difference, God has no favorites—made no modifications in my gospel." In other words, they did not insist that Gentile converts should undergo circumcision and bind themselves to keep the Law.

On the contrary (2:7-9), convinced that God was "using" Paul in his evangelical work among the Gentiles just as truly as he was "using" Peter to convert the Jews, the three leaders unhesitatingly gave Paul and Barnabas their blessing and bade them "God-speed" in their work among the Gentiles. "Pillars"—the name Paul gives James, Cephas, and John—is a common metaphor in all languages to indicate the important people in a community.

At this meeting, Paul goes on to say (2:9-10), spheres of influence were assigned. The Jerusalem Apostles agreed that, while they themselves should stick to home missions, as we would say, Paul and Barnabas should go to the foreign field. But they made one request, that Paul and Barnabas should remember the poor Christians of the Jerusalem mother Church. (The name "Ebionites" or "poor ones" seems to have been applied to the Jerusalem Church even before it was given to some early sects of Jewish heretics.) "Which very thing," Paul comments, "I was eager to do." Was it not precisely on just such an errand that Barnabas and he had come up to Jerusalem? How important Paul considered his "collection for the saints," his later letters witness. The gathering and delivery of it was a prime concern of Paul's during the whole third missionary journey (Rom. 15:25-29; I Cor. 16:1-4; II Cor. 8; Acts 24:17).

The Clash Between Paul and Peter at Antioch (2:11-21)

Now, quite abruptly, Paul refers to an occasion when he clashed with Peter at Antioch. (Antioch in Syria, the third city of the Roman Empire, was the cradle of Gentile Christianity and Paul's base of operations for his great missionary journeys.) When did this collision, which is not recorded in Acts, take place? The probable answer is that it came between Paul's second visit to Jerusalem, which we have just been discussing, and the Apostolic Council in Jerusalem, generally dated in A.D. 49. Sometime, then, in the late "forties" Peter had left Jerusalem to visit Antioch. On his arrival, realizing the true meaning of Christian freedom, he had sat down to meals with the Gentile Christians, thus showing that he knew Christ had abolished all barriers between Jews and Gentiles. But one day the arrival of some men from James in Jerusalem—these would be Jewish Christians with more rigid views—had caused consternation in the Antioch Church. Thereupon, afraid of appearing lax before the Jerusalem brethren, Peter had reverted to his old Jewish scruples about eating with Gentiles, and had left them to take their meals alone. His bad example was followed by the rest of the Jewish Christians and even by Barnabas, Paul's colleague in the Gentile mission field. Paul, therefore, took his courage in his hands and publicly remonstrated with Peter. A vital issue of the gospel was in grave jeopardy, and no compromise was possible for Paul. It is a great thing in life to know when such a moment is on us—one thinks of Luther at Worms—and to stand then like a rock. Paul knew, as he puts it, that "they were not on the right road to the truth of the gospel" (so literally 2:14), and he told Peter so, quite bluntly, before them all. "Why," he said to Peter, "this complete rightabout-face? You used to eat with our Gentile brothers, you accepted Gentile standards of living and felt no obligation to maintain Jewish practice. How utterly inconsistent of you now to ask Gentiles to accept the same Jewish ways of living which everyone knows you discarded!"

Of course Paul was right, and the occasion quite momentous. If Paul had sided with Peter and compromised, Jewish Christianity and Gentile Christianity would have gone their own separate ways, and the ideal of one Church of the living God, one Body of Christ, would have been stifled at birth! But might not a private rebuke of Peter have been wiser? Do not public quarrels of this kind between ecclesiastical leaders do untold damage to the Church's cause? Perhaps; but in this case the wrong had been public and was notorious, and the only remedy was a public remonstrance.

Verse 14 gives us the actual words Paul used; the following verses give the general drift of the argument with which he supported his protest. What is very interesting in this argument is the identity of opinion assumed between Peter and Paul. It is taken for granted, not only that Peter is a Christian but that he is a Christian of a *Pauline* type. We sometimes suppose that the doctrine of "justification by faith" is Paul's own peculiar contribution to the gospel. Here Paul makes it quite clear that it was something which all Christians held, that is, the view that one's acceptance with God does not come by works of law—by trying to lay up a credit balance of good deeds in the ledgers of heaven —but by trusting in Christ who has died for our sins. When, knowing ourselves to be sinners who cannot perfectly keep God's law, we put our trust in the Son of God who died to redeem us, God accepts us for Christ's sake, grants us his forgiveness, and sets our feet on the way to salvation.

We may now paraphrase Paul's argument in verses 15 and 16. "We are agreed, you and I, Peter—both of us Jews, mark you, and not 'Gentile sinners,' as Jewry scornfully names them— that there is only one way to get right with God, and that is by trusting in Christ and not by trying to keep the Law. If, then, we who are Jewish Christians, who have found salvation in this way, now insist that Gentile Christians conform to the Law, we are cutting the ground from beneath our own feet. We are recommending a way of salvation which we both know to be a blind alley." And Paul, as is his wont, appeals to the words of Scripture to clinch his point. The Scripture quoted is Psalm 143:2; but Paul adds here, as he does in Romans 3:20, the significant phrase not found in the Psalmist, "by works of the law" (2:16).

But Paul's argument with Peter is not yet quite over. The sense of the difficult two verses that follow (2:17-18) is this: "You and I, Peter, who are Jews, by renouncing the Law and trusting in Christ for salvation, put ourselves on the same level as Gentile sinners. Now you, Peter, by returning to the Law, are implying that we acted wrongly. Yet who led you along this road to Christian freedom? Was it not Christ himself? Was it not he who inspired you to fraternize with the Gentiles, an action which you now apparently regard as sinful? So you make Christ responsible for sin! This is completely absurd. No, no! It is the man who goes back to the Law who is the sinner. By reverting to your legalism, Peter, you are re-establishing what your Christian conscience has outgrown. And is that not sinful?"

With the next verse (2:19) Paul moves away from the crisis at Antioch to the great crisis in his own life. "For I through the law died to the law, that I might live to God." Paul has just said that the sin lies in going back to the Law after it has been abandoned. In fact, he now adds, it was the Law itself which led him to abandon it. In other words, his experience under the Law revealed to him how ineffective the Law was to save. What it did was to awaken in him the consciousness of sin, and so it led him to renounce the Law as a way of salvation and to turn to Christ. So he "died to the law"; that is, at his conversion all that characterized his old life, all his old ideals and ambitions, simply fell away and ceased to matter, for through Christ he had found what he had been seeking, the true way of living for God.

And with this Paul turns in the last two verses of the chapter (2:20-21) to describe his new life. First, and negatively, it is said to be a crucifixion to the old life. "When I was converted," he says in effect, "it was as if I had been nailed, along with Christ, to the cross. The old life, the old friends, the old habits, were forever and completely behind me. And what was the result? There is a new life, so closely lived in communion with the risen Lord that it is as if my own ego, or self, had gone out of me, and in its place had come Christ to take up his abode." Here theological interpretation fails, and only personal experience will enable us to understand. Here is Pauline mysticism, but not his alone. Does not every man, who is suddenly and wonderfully converted from an old evil life, know what Paul is describing here? There is nothing magical about this life, as Paul goes on to say, since it is based completely on faith. "The life I now live in the flesh I live by faith in the Son of God, who loved me and gave himself for me." Faith, as this verse makes plain, is not the act of a moment only, it is the attitude of a whole life. It is not to say one time, "I believe in Christ"; it is to go on, day after day, month after month, year after year, believing with all one's heart in Christ as God's Son, who so loved us as to give his life for us. Here is the fact of the Atonement again. But note how Paul appropriates to himself the love that belongs to the whole world. With the last verse (2:21) we return to the dispute with the Judaizers. To go back now to the Law, Paul says, would be to refuse the incomparable grace of God in the Cross. Going back to the Law would imply that it really could save. And this would mean that there was no need for Christ to die—"Christ died to no purpose."

THE DOCTRINAL ARGUMENT

Galatians 3:1—4:31

The Appeal to Experience (3:1-5)

The historical retrospect is over. Now, in chapters 3 and 4, Paul faces his readers with the doctrinal issue—Christ, or the Law? First, he will appeal to experience, then to Scripture, and finally to reason.

"O foolish Galatians! Who has bewitched you . . . ?" (3:1). The Galatians are, of course, Paul's converts in the Roman province of Galatia (see the Introduction). The Greek verb rendered "bewitched" suggests the act of a sorcerer in "casting an evil eye" on his victim. No doubt Paul uses it metaphorically, as we nowadays use "fascinate" (which means literally "cast the evil eye on"). "Who has hypnotized you?" might be our modern equivalent. In the words, "before whose eyes Jesus Christ was publicly portrayed as crucified," the reference to "eyes" catches up the metaphor of the evil eye. The evil eye could take effect only if the victim met the sorcerer's gaze. If, Paul says in effect, the Galatians had only kept their gaze steadily fixed on the living Crucified, whom he had preached as Savior, they would have been immune to the spells of the Judaizing brethren. "Publicly portrayed" is, in Greek, literally "placarded," like an advertisement on a billboard. The image conveys the graphic way Paul had told the story of the Cross to them. Perhaps a great hymn like "When I Survey the Wondrous Cross" will suggest what his preaching must have been like. The Greek word rendered "crucified" is a construction which expresses a past event whose results abide into the present. The Cross is not a mere *past* fact, but a *present* reality, daily felt by men. (From the amount of space given to the story of the Cross in the Gospels we know that the early Christians were trained to know it in this way.)

Then comes the appeal to experience (3:2), ever the most effective of Christian arguments: "Did you receive the Spirit by doing what the Law commanded, or by believing the gospel message?" Notice that the New Testament never asks, "Do you believe in the Holy Spirit?" The question is always, "Did you receive the Holy Spirit?" (see Acts 19:2). Paul's point here is clear. None could gainsay the wonderful new spiritual life which had come to the Galatians. They had experienced that "uprush of life," with all its sense of fellowship, with its new access of power and joy and hope, which was the infallible sign of the presence of God's Holy Spirit. How had this come about? By keeping the Law or by hearing the gospel with faith? To ask the question was to answer it. Of course law-keeping had nothing to do with it.

Then (3:3) Paul puts a second question, which we may paraphrase: "Do you not find something incongruous in beginning with moving spiritual experiences and ending up with external trivialities like the flesh, that is, circumcision?" He goes on in verse 4: "Did you experience so many things in vain?" He is saying, "Have you had all these wonderful spiritual experiences for nothing?" The expression, "if it really is in vain," indicates that Paul is unwilling to believe the worst of his converts. After all, did he not write elsewhere, "Love . . . believes all things," implying "all good things"? (I Cor. 13:7).

Paul's final question (3:5) repeats verse 2. "Tell me, please, how came this lavish supply of spiritual gifts from God? Was it the result of law-keeping or of dynamic faith?" "He who supplies the Spirit to you and works miracles among you" is God, and the reference to miracles reminds us that, just as Jesus had wrought miracles, so did many of his first followers. They wrought them in the name of Jesus (see, for an example, Acts 3:6) and they ascribed them to the power of the Holy Spirit (see Rom. 15:19, "signs and wonders, by the power of the Holy Spirit"). If we had more of "the faith that rebels" and more reliance on the Holy Spirit, we, too, might work many wonders!

The Faith of Abraham (3:6-9)

Having appealed to experience, Paul now appeals to Scripture. His argument is that faith, not works, is the way to acceptance with God. So he points to "father Abraham" who, for the Jew, was not only the founder of the race but the righteous man par excellence. How did *he* find favor with God? "Consult your Bibles," says Paul, "and the answer will be plain. Abraham found favor with God because of his faith" (see Gen. 15:6). To claim Abraham for his case was to steal the Judaizers' thunder with a vengeance. They wanted to go back to the Law of Moses. Paul takes them back further still, to the faith of Abraham. There, in the beginning of the story of salvation, he says, you find that faith is the way to acceptance with God. Christians, therefore, whose relation with God is based on faith, are Abraham's true descendants, truer to his type than are circumcised Jews. For, Paul adds (3:8), there is a real anticipation of the gospel in the Old Testament. "The scripture . . . preached the gospel beforehand to Abraham, saying, 'In thee shall all the nations be blessed.'" The point here seems to be this: God's gracious dealing with Abraham, as recorded in the Genesis story, which stressed *promise* on the part of God and answering *faith* on the part of Abraham, involves the root-principle of the Christian gospel, which means taking God at his word in Christ, just as Abraham similarly took God at his word. Therefore (3:9) all men of faith stand together, because they stand in direct line from father Abraham, the true pioneer of the relationship of faith.

Does the reader find this kind of argument oversubtle and unconvincing? It is undoubtedly the type of argument used by rabbis or Jewish teachers of Paul's day. But let us not miss Paul's main point, which is that the great souls of the Old Testament like Abraham had a relationship with God which was deeper and more real than anything which keeping the Law has to offer. Faith, Paul would teach us, is something which did not begin with the New Testament but lies deep at the heart of all biblical religion.

The Curse of the Law (3:10-14)

Paul now attacks the very Law on which his opponents relied. Still using his prooftexts from the Old Testament in the manner approved at the time, he shows that, whereas the Law can only bring us into condemnation, faith in Christ brings us deliverance.

The Law, Paul begins, cannot be the way to salvation, because instead of God's promised blessing it brings only a curse on all who fail to keep its provisions fully, as Deuteronomy 27:26 says. Paul assumes in verse 10, be it noted, that all men are sinful, a point which he argues out in the Letter to the Romans.

Since, then, on the basis of Law no man can find favor with God, salvation must come on a different basis, namely, the basis of faith, as Habakkuk 2:4 says: "He who through faith is righteous shall live," that is, be saved. (It should be noted that for Habakkuk faith meant "steadfastness.") But the Law does not deal with *faith* but with *actions,* imposing on us the impossible task of fulfilling all its rules and regulations, as Leviticus 18:5 indicates: "He who *does* them shall live by them." This proves to be an illusory promise of life indeed, since no man can *do* them all! (3:11-12).

Thus, apart from Christ, we are lost. But from this curse of death Christ has set us free by dying a death declared by the Law itself to be a typical example of the curse in action (see Deut. 21:23). Christ acted as our representative; by taking the Law's curse on himself, he rendered it null and void, so that we go free. Christ's death is regarded here as both representative and penal, that is, he acted in our place and took upon himself the penalty due to us. This is similar to what Paul says about the Cross in II Corinthians 5:21 where Christ is said to have been "made . . . to be sin" for us. Whatever we make of it, we cannot deny that Paul holds a doctrine of the Atonement which gives warrant to the term "penal substitution." We may not say, of course, that Christ was personally accursed, but we must say that he, as our representative, endured all that is involved in being a member of a doomed race (3:13).

What did his atoning death achieve? He put an end to the reign of Law by exhausting its curse. In this way he fulfilled the original plan of God, according to which the blessing was promised to Abraham's spiritual descendants through faith. Thus, salvation is now available for Gentiles who through faith obtain the promised blessing, the Holy Spirit (3:14).

The Law's Purpose: Not to Annul the Promise but to Expose Sin (3:15-22)

Still discussing the Law and the Promise, Paul now employs a human illustration. Since the section is difficult, Paul's thought should be put in the simplest terms.

"Take a human agreement," he says. "Once it is duly ratified, nobody can annul it. Now, if this is true of a human agreement, how much more true it is of a divine one! A divine agreement will surely stand. Such was God's promise to Abraham. Look at the wording of it. It was given, says the Scripture, to a single person, not to many—to Abraham's *offspring* (singular), not to his *offsprings* (plural). The person meant here is Christ, and of course, by implication, those who are Christ's. Now the Law, which came four centuries after the time of Abraham, cannot possibly set aside this earlier agreement, the promise. Consider this: the blessing cannot come both ways, by law *and* by promise. If it depends on keeping the Law, the promise would be inoperative; but God chose to give it the gracious way, by promise" (see 3:15-18).

What, then, was the distinctive function of the Law? It was a temporary measure, introduced to expose sin as transgression, and it was valid only until the true inheritor of the promise, Christ, arrived. Besides, since the Law was given through angels and a human mediator (Moses), it bears the marks of inferiority. How unlike the case of Abraham to whom God spoke face to face! (3:19-20).

You must not, therefore, infer that the Law is *opposed* to the promise. But the Law could not give life. Had it been able to do this, legalism would have been the way of salvation. As it was, Scripture consigned all men into the same pen of sin, to show that there was but one way left—the way of "faith in Jesus Christ" (3:21-22).

Now a few points of detail in the passage should be examined. In verse 15 the Revised Standard Version has the word "will" for a Greek word which, in the Greek Old Testament, normally translates the Hebrew word for "covenant." For this reason the word "agreement" appears in the paraphrase above.

Paul's handling of Scripture in verse 16 may seem like verbal hairsplitting. But the argument is theologically defensible, since for Paul, Christ is a *corporate* person, mankind's representative before God.

In 3:17 the figure of 430 years comes from the Greek translation of Exodus 12:40 in the Septuagint. In 3:19 we meet the Jewish tradition also based on the Septuagint version (Deut. 33:2), that the Law was transmitted to men through angels (see Acts 7:38 and Heb. 2:2).

It has been said that there are 250 to 300 interpretations of verse 20! The most natural meaning seems to be: mediation implies two parties; the Law, being a contract, is valid so long as both sides fulfill the conditions; but God, the giver of the promise, is one; thus there are not two parties to the promise, which is absolute and unconditional.

What "scripture" is meant in verse 22? Paul must have in his mind various passages agreeing with one another, such as he quotes in Romans 3:10-18 to prove the universal sinfulness of man.

One last comment is necessary. Does this passage, arguing in the fashion of the rabbis, contain any permanent truth? Surely it does. What Paul is saying is that *promise,* not *law,* is fundamental in God's dealing with us. From the story of God's dealings with Abraham in Genesis we may see, Paul insists, what God is like. Once gracious, he is always gracious.

The Law Our Custodian (3:23-29)

Up till now Paul has been ruthlessly exposing the inadequacies of the Law. Had it, then, no place in the divine plan? Yes, answers Paul in the verses that follow. It was a necessary discipline on the road to our promised inheritance in the gospel, which is sonship in Christ. God, so to speak, appointed the Law as a kind of guardian, to restrain us until the coming of Christian salvation. In fact, says Paul, you might compare the Law to a "pedagogue," that is, the household servant who took care of children when young, conducted them to and from school, and generally disciplined them until they came of age. (The word "custodian" in verse 24 is probably the best English equivalent for the Greek word here, though even it is inadequate. The older rendering, "schoolmaster," will not do; it is the disciplinary, not the educative, purpose of the Law which Paul has in mind.)

However, since faith in Christ has now become a glad reality, we no longer need the services of our custodian (3:24-25). Hitherto having the status of wards, we have now become, in Christ, "sons of God, through faith" (3:26). The seal on such faith was baptism, to whose significance Paul now refers (3:27): "For as many of you as were baptized into Christ have put on Christ." What does the phrase "baptized into" mean? When a convert, confessing that "Jesus is Lord," was baptized, he was held to pass into Christ's possession, to become Christ's man. So close was the faith-union thus established and sealed, that he could be said to have "put on Christ," as though Christ were a garment. (So, in much the same way, the Old Testament speaks of being clothed with righteousness.) Henceforth such a man began to take on something of Christ's character and became, indeed, a new man! When this happens to people, Paul goes on to say, the old distinctions of class and caste go by the board, or ought to! "There is neither Jew nor Greek, there is neither slave nor free, there is neither male nor female." Shall we put this in modern terms: "In the Christian society there can be no place for white or black, management or labor, man or woman." "For you are all one in Christ Jesus" (3:28); that is, you stand, each one of you, on the same level as your neighbors in the society of Christ. Being Christ's people, then, you must also be "Abraham's offspring"—Christ being *the* true inheritor of the promise to Abraham. The promise made to Abraham is, therefore, fulfilled in Christ's people, who are the true heirs of God's Kingdom (3:29).

Freedom as Sons (4:1-7)

Still dwelling on the idea of "heir," Paul resorts to a legal analogy. "Till he reaches the age fixed by his father," he says, "an heir is a minor with no rights. During this time of tutelage he is subject to guardians, who care for his person, and trustees, who look after his property. Then one day, his minorship over, he comes into his own. So, spiritually speaking, it was with us. While we were minors, our life was a slavish subjection to the elemental spirits. Then came the time of our emancipation" (4: 1-3).

Some doubt surrounds the law about minors which is presupposed in the first two verses, although I Maccabees 3:32-33 and 6:17 offer a parallel in treating the status of the heir of a Syrian ruler. But Paul's meaning is clear, even if he changes his metaphor at verse 4. The Law fulfilled its appointed purpose of restraint and discipline till it pleased God to end our tutelage and make us his sons and heirs. Verse 3 contains an important point. "We were slaves," Paul says, "to the elemental spirits of the universe." Once it was thought that Paul was here describing Gentile and Jewish religion before Christ came, as a kind of religious ABC, or the rudimentary forms of religion. But the way Paul talks about these "elements" later in this chapter and in Colossians 2:8, 20 leads most modern interpreters to understand the "elements" as the heavenly bodies and the spirit-powers which were thought to inhabit them and to control men's destinies. Pagan men in these days did believe their destinies to be at the mercy of such sinister heavenly powers. But it is hardly less doubtful that many Jews did much the same. We know that they linked the Law with angelic beings (3:19). Furthermore, the Jewish festivals, about whose observance the Galatians were so fussy (4:10), were fixed by the movements of the heavenly bodies. Thus Paul can lump both the Law ritual of the Jews and the idolatry of the Gentiles together, calling them alike slavery to these elemental powers. Such, he says, were your guardians till Christ came.

"But when the time had fully come" (4:4), Christ came and changed everything. The *time*, which is "the date set by the father" (4:2)—our Heavenly Father—is the right time determined by God in his inscrutable wisdom. From our human angle we can see, however, how propitious circumstances were for the great Event, with the Jewish Law, the common Greek language, and the Roman peace. Then "God sent forth his Son," Paul says, clearly conceiving Christ as a divine Being, filially related to the Almighty, existing with him before he appeared in time. (See also Romans 8:3, and Mark 12:1-12 where in parabolic form the sending of the Son is described.)

The phrase, "born of woman," asserts the full humanity of the Son, as "born under the law" suggests a birthplace, providentially arranged, so that the Son might learn sympathy with sinners and those in bondage. For he came to "redeem those who were under the law" (4:5); that is, to "buy them out" of bondage to the Law by enduring and exhausting in himself the curse of the Law (3:13). The end in view was our adoption as sons (4:5). The metaphor comes from the Graeco-Roman (but not Jewish) legal device whereby a wealthy childless man might take into his family a slave youth who thus, by a great stroke of fortune, ceased to be a slave and became a son and heir. This particular figure Paul uses to show that we are sons by grace, whereas Christ is a Son by nature.

How do we know that we are sons? Because, answers Paul, the Holy Spirit in our hearts moves us to approach God as children to a father (4:6; see also Rom. 8:15). *"Abba"* had been Jesus' own word of address to God. An Aramaic word, it was used by the Jewish child in talking to his earthly father (somewhat like our "Daddy"); but no pious Jew would have dreamt of addressing God thus familiarly. Only one Man did so (Mark 14:36), and he taught his disciples to do likewise (Luke 11:2, where "Father" translates a word which is equivalent to *Abba*). The Lord's usage had so hallowed the Aramaic word that the Church took it over. But why "Abba! Father!" (the Aramaic word, with its Greek equivalent following it)? It looks as if Paul would not allow one word in a foreign tongue without adding a translation —admirable common sense! (Just possibly the word came into the Church through the corporate use of the Lord's Prayer whose first word, in Luke's version, is "Father.") Here, then, we touch the rich heart of Christian experience. And is not the longing to approach God as Father a witness to the yearning of the spirit made in God's image which knows no rest until it rests in him? Verse 7 sums up. No longer slaves, we are sons and heirs, by God's own act given free access to all the riches he destines for us.

Warning Against Relapse (4:8-11)

Paul stands aghast that men privileged to know God as Father through Christ his Son should ever dream of turning back to this sorry slavish paganism. The beings they had once served so slavishly were no gods at all. (Note: he does not deny their existence; he denies that they are divine.) Such conduct passes comprehension in men who had once come to know the true God or, rather, had come to be known by him. The antithesis is important. We find it also in I Corinthians 8:3 and I Corinthians 13:12. Always Paul sees the divine initiative in the work of man's salvation. Does man seek God? Then it is because God is already seeking him. Does man love him? Then it is because God loved him first. How, then, can men who have known God in this way, lapse back again into a worship of spiritual powers which are "weak" because they cannot save them, and "beggarly" because they ill become the rich heirs of God? Then (4:10) he attacks their fussy observance of Jewish sabbaths, new moons, annual feasts, and sabbatical years, probably because such observances were closely tied up with the idolatrous worship of the stars and their potentates. But did not Paul himself observe the main Jewish feasts, and did he not recognize the Lord's Day? Yes, but what Paul condemns is not the celebration of the high days in the religious calendar, but a fussy, all-absorbing concentration on times and seasons, dedicated to quite undivine deities. If Paul's converts prefer this mummery to the adoration of Abba, Father, his work among them has gone for nought.

Let us not say that this kind of thing has never happened, or could never happen now, among Christians. The Galatians are not so very different from some Christians, who exchange the rich realities of a truly evangelical Christianity for an obsession with saints' days or with pagan rituals of one kind or another.

A Personal Appeal (4:12-20)

Paul interrupts his doctrinal argument to make a moving personal appeal. He recalls how his first visit to Galatia (recorded in Acts 13 and 14) had been due to a physical illness which had befallen him. Doubtless the "thorn in the flesh" (II Cor. 12:7) refers to the same trouble. What was it? Ophthalmia (an inflammatory condition of the eye)? Epilepsy? Both guesses have had their supporters. But the best conjecture is that Paul contracted malaria in the swampy coastlands of Pamphylia and, to recuperate, went inland to the highlands of Galatia. In his sick state even his physical appearance must have been a trial to them, he says; yet, instead of despising him, they welcomed him like a messenger from heaven. The allusion is to Acts 14:11-12 when the Galatians in Lystra received Paul as Hermes, the "messenger" or "angel" (in Greek the two words mean the same thing) of the gods. At the time the Galatians had behaved very much like a church which has secured the services of a popular pastor. They went about saying how very "fortunate" they were. Well, asks Paul, "what has become of the satisfaction you felt" then? (What happened in Paul's case should be a warning to all modern churches not to place too much importance on the personal tie between man and man!) Those who think Paul's eyesight was bad, point to the phrase about "plucking out their eyes" as proof. But it may be no more than a graphic phrase describing a deep affection.

But the Galatians had undergone a change of face. Was it caused by his telling them the truth? Paul asks this, and goes on to warn them against the actual designs of the Judaizers (4:17-18). "Of course they are courting you—for their own selfish ends," he is saying. What he means when he says to them, "[The Judaizers] want to shut you out," is not quite clear. The sense of verse 18 seems to be: "Don't think I am jealous of the attention you are now receiving." Then the appeal climaxes with a burst of affection: "My little children"—a phrase found only here in Paul, but a favorite with John. The imagery of 4:19 seems a bit unorthodox, for it is Paul who undergoes the labor, and they are expected to produce the child! But the thought is moving and powerful: "Must I go through all the hard travail once again in order that Christ may reincarnate himself in your hearts? Ah, if I could only talk to you face to face and adjust my tones to suit your situation!" In such a situation it is clear that a personal interview is better than a long-range correspondence.

The Allegory of Sarah and Hagar (4:21-31)

To confound the enthusiasts for the Law, using the Law itself and the case of Abraham their spiritual forefather—this is what Paul now attempts. The result is his allegory of Sarah and Hagar.

Abraham had two sons: Ishmael, the son of the slavewoman Hagar, was born in the ordinary course of nature; and Isaac, son of the freewoman Sarah, was born following a divine promise when Sarah seemed too old to have a family.

Now, Paul explains, there is a deep meaning in this story. The two women with their sons symbolize two covenants, or dispensations. Hagar, mother of the despised Ishmaelites, represents the Sinai Covenant, as her outcast children represent the Jews in bondage to the Law. Sarah, however, represents the

New Covenant, and her children are the men of faith, Jew and Gentile, who live for freedom.

This is the meaning of verses 21-26, in which Paul's aim is to show from Scripture that God planned to replace the Law and the Old Covenant of Sinai by a New Covenant of freedom. Notice that Sarah is identified (4:26) with "the Jerusalem above," a figure for the Christian Church, seen in its ideal form, whose destiny begins and ends in heaven. To strengthen his argument (4:27), Paul quotes Isaiah 54:1, the point of which is the fruitfulness of the Christian Church after the long period of barrenness when the Law held sway and limited God's people to the Jews.

Then another point of correspondence strikes Paul (4:29). He has just said that we Christians are like Isaac, the "children of promise," when he recalls the old Jewish legend that Ishmael's "mocking" of Isaac (Gen. 21:9) took the form of "persecuting" him (Ishmael was said to have shot at Isaac with a bow). Was not this a prefigurement in Scripture of what was happening in the Jewish persecution of the Christians?

The allegory comes to its climax in verse 30. You remember, says Paul, the end of the Hagar story in Genesis and the command that was given: "Cast Hagar and Ishmael out and do not let them inherit along with Sarah and her son" (see Gen. 21:10-12). Is not this clear proof from Scripture that the exclusion of the Jews from the Kingdom of God is divinely decreed?

That is the allegory with its stern conclusion. Again the form of argument is, through and through, like that used by the rabbis, and we may find it too arbitrary to be convincing. We also remember that in Romans 11 Paul had what seem to be second, and finer, thoughts about the final destiny of the Jews. Yet, strangely as the allegory strikes us, the thrilling fact remains that the gospel of freedom is as old as Abraham.

THE PRACTICAL APPLICATION
Galatians 5:1—6:10

Choose Freedom (5:1-12)

"Whatever you do," Paul begins, "never surrender the freedom Christ has won for you! Never bow your necks again under the yoke of slavery" (5:1). Then he attacks circumcision on two counts.

First (5:2-3), it binds a man to keep the whole Jewish Law. "You cannot decide to submit to circumcision," he says in effect, "and still put your whole trust in Christ. Let yourself be circumcised, and you must keep the Law in its entirety."

Second (5:4-5), obedience to the Law separates a man from Christ. Why? Because it stands for a religious principle quite different from the principle of faith, and it puts a man outside Christ and outside the pale of God's grace. Paul goes on to say that "we," that is, those of us who trust to Christ alone for salvation, cherish "the hope of righteousness"—acceptance with God —as much as anybody; but we look for it to come "through the Spirit" (not through the Law) and "by faith" (not by works). Verse 6 sums up this section—and indeed the message of Galatians—in one of Paul's great sentences: "For in Christ Jesus neither circumcision nor uncircumcision is of any avail, but faith working through love." What this means is this: "In any proper Christ-centered Christianity the thing that matters is not any external rite—or the absence of it—but trust in Christ as Savior, outflowing in a life of love." Here is the Magna Charta of any truly evangelical Christianity! And note how closely akin Paul and James are in the light of it. The faith that James denounces in his letter is one that does not issue in deeds of love. The faith that Paul praises is one that cannot help expressing itself in love.

In verses 7-12 Paul turns from circumcision to the circumcisers themselves. The Galatians had been making splendid progress until this setback arose. "Who cut in on you," asks Paul, using a familiar metaphor (5:7), "so that your progress was suddenly halted?" Paul supplies the answer to his own question: No doubt some bad influence from outside intervened. "A little yeast," he says, "leavens the whole lump" (5:9; see I Cor. 5:6). But he is sure that eventually they will come round to his own view, and the ringleader in the trouble, whoever he is, will get his deserts. Then, suddenly, he recalls a charge which his enemies were circulating. They were saying—though it almost staggers belief—that Paul was still preaching circumcision. "If this is really true," Paul retorts, "is it not odd that I am highly unpopular with the Jews?" (5:11). In that case, he adds ironically, the Cross of Christ has lost all its value for salvation, if the Law is all you need in order to be saved. And he ends very bitterly: "These trouble-makers love cutting. I wish they would do it thoroughly and castrate themselves!" (Some of the priests of the

Asian goddess Cybele practiced castration as a part of their worship.)

Not License but Love, Not Flesh but Spirit (5:13-26)

What kind of life is expected of those who have been justified by faith and who enjoy Christian freedom? The answer is: a life that is free and holy and loving, because it is informed by the Spirit of a gracious God. Such freedom is not liberty to do as one likes; it is freedom to act in love through the Spirit's power.

"Beware," Paul begins (5:13), "of supposing that Christian freedom means the end of all moral restraints." An old jingle well summarizes this fallacy (which is known as "antinomianism"):

> Free from the Law!
> O happy condition!
> I can sin as I please
> And still have remission.

On the contrary, Paul says, freedom means service. "Through love be servants of one another" (5:13). Quoting Leviticus 19:18 (as his Lord had done), he declares that a man who loves his neighbor fulfills the whole Law. In other words, the life of loving service fulfills the real intention that underlies the Law (see Mark 12:29-31 and Rom. 13:8-10). To snap and bite at one another, as some of them are doing, is to ruin themselves (5:15).

In verses 16-26 Paul says, "Live the life of the Spirit, and shun the deeds of the flesh." By the "Spirit" he means the new, supernatural power of God, available for all Christians since the Day of Pentecost (Acts 2). By the "flesh" he means our unregenerate lower nature, with all its unlovely appetites and impulses—human nature as tainted by sin and apart from the grace of God. Between these two, Spirit and flesh, there is a steady and relentless tug of war, and it is the Christian's duty to see that his life is controlled by the Spirit. When Paul says (5:17) that flesh and Spirit "are opposed to each other, to prevent you from doing what you would," he means that the downward pulls and pressures of our lower nature prevent us from obeying the dictates of our conscience. "But," he adds, "if you are led by the Spirit you are not under the law" (5:18). The Spirit-controlled man is delivered from the terrible conflict of the man under the Law, so movingly described by Paul in Romans 7.

The things done by our lower nature are plain to see (5:19),
and there follows a catalogue of fifteen "works of the flesh,"
ranging from sexual sin to drunkenness, and including idolatry
and sorcery (5:19-21). They may be classified as sexual sins
(immorality, impurity, and licentiousness); pagan sins (idolatry
and sorcery); sins of faction (enmity, strife, jealousy, anger,
selfishness, dissension, party spirit, and envy); and sins of ap-
petite (drunkenness and carousing). Against these vices Paul had
repeatedly warned them (when he was in Galatia); he now
reiterates his warning that people who indulge in these things
"shall not inherit the kingdom of God"; that is, they will forfeit
their chance of final salvation (5:21).

Such are the deeds of the flesh. What the Spirit produces is
nine lovely virtues: "love, joy, peace, patience, kindness, goodness, faithfulness, gentleness, self-control" (5:22-23), all characteristically Christian qualities, with love at their head, so that,
as somebody has said, the fruits of the Spirit are the virtues of
Christ. The very word "fruit" (or "harvest") suggests that these
lovely virtues are the *outflowering* of the indwelling Spirit of
God.

First comes "love," which means "caring" for other people;
then "joy," which is not merely *joie de vivre,* but the deep conviction, born of God, that life means good; then "peace," that
serenity of mind springing from a right relationship with God;
then "patience," or "long temper," which is the happy opposite
of "short temper"; then "kindness"; then "goodness," which is
righteousness informed by love; then "faith," that is, fidelity or
reliability; then "gentleness," or considerateness for others; and
finally, "self-control," which is a word of far wider scope than
our "temperance."

Then Paul adds the comment: "And those who belong to
Christ Jesus have crucified the flesh with its passions and desires"
(5:24). Just as Christ in the flesh overcame the power of the
fleshly principle, so those who are bound to him by faith are, in
principle at least, finished with all that belongs to the flesh. Theirs
is, or ought to be, the power of the Spirit. "Very well then," Paul
concludes, "if the Holy Spirit is really the inner principle of your
lives, see that you shape your outward acts according to it. And
let us have no more of that conceit and provoking of one another
which have marred your fellowship" (see 5:25-26).

Sundry Christian Counsels (6:1-10)

What does Christian love mean in actual practice? Perhaps because he had heard of some harsh judgment passed on a Christian brother in the Galatian church, Paul now gives an example. "Suppose one of you is caught in some trespass," he says, "act as men inspired by the Spirit (not by the Law), and deal with him gently, remembering that none of us is immune to temptation." The word "restore" translates a Greek verb derived from medical language and used of "setting" a broken bone. It suggests that in our Christian dealing with men we should try to be constructive, not destructive. By so bearing one another's burdens of moral failure and the like, the Galatians will be fulfilling the law of Christ, that is, acting according to Christ's precepts and commands. "The law of Christ" here means Christ's moral teaching which supplies a design for Christian living. Whether any of it was written down as early as this is not certain.

In verse 3 Paul warns his readers against an overweening conceit of themselves. One cause of spiritual pride is the bad habit of comparing ourselves with others—to *their* disadvantage. The cure for this is a ruthless self-scrutiny. "For each man will have to bear his own load" (6:5). In verse 2 the Greek word for "burden" means a weight. In verse 5 the word "load" is a word sometimes used of a soldier's kit. It represents that *load* of personal responsibility which each man must shoulder for himself, and for which God will hold him accountable at the Judgment Day.

At this point (6:6), rather abruptly, Paul puts in a plea for what might be called "the maintenance of the ministry." We know that Paul had appointed elders in South Galatia (Acts 14:23). This verse proves that the church there had Christian teachers who drew no salary. Just as Paul elsewhere (I Cor. 9:14) insists that "those who proclaim the gospel should get their living by the gospel," so here he commands their pupils or "catechumens" to share their (material) goods with their teachers.

Then he strikes a stern note (6:7). Let them not delude themselves into thinking that, because they are sons of God rejoicing in their freedom from the Law, they have to deal with an easygoing Deity, who will suspend his eternal laws for their special benefit. "God is not to be sneered at," he says in effect—using a Greek verb which means "turn up one's nose at"—"he sees to it that a man reaps what he sows." If he "sows to his own flesh," that is, to his lower nature, it will bring him a ruinous harvest. If he "sows to the Spirit," that is, lets the Holy Spirit control his life, the reward will be "eternal life," that wonderful new quality of life lived in communion with God, to be begun here and to be perfected hereafter (6:8).

Indefatigable well-doing, therefore, is our appointed duty, and we may rest assured that if we do not falter or fail, in due season—in God's good time—we shall be recompensed (6:9). The sum of the matter is that we are to miss no chance of doing good to all men, remembering especially the "household of faith" (6:10); that is, the children in God's family, the members of the Church. This is the Christian version of the proverb which says that "charity begins at home."

AUTOGRAPH POSTCRIPT
Galatians 6:11-18

It was Paul's habit to dictate his letters to an amanuensis and to append, at the last, his own signature to authenticate the whole letter. But in Galatians, when he takes the pen from the amanuensis, he adds not merely his signature but eight verses of autograph postscript, because he has something very important to say in conclusion. This is the meaning of the "large letters" in his own hand. We would say nowadays "in bold capitals," and we would use them to emphasize what we had to say.

The postscript, in fact, contains his final solemn warning to his converts in Galatia not to be deceived and hoodwinked by the Judaizers. Behind their concern for your circumcision, Paul says, lie the desire to appear to be good orthodox Jews and the desire to escape the persecution which will befall them if they proclaim Christ crucified as God's appointed way of saving sinners (6:12). But even these Judaizers themselves do not keep the Law; their only concern is to swell the number of their proselytes, which is a kind of fleshly glorying. That kind of success story has no appeal for Paul. His only wish to glory is in the Cross of Christ which, when a man truly appropriates its virtue, brings his old life to a close and separates him forever from the world.

Then comes one of Paul's great summarizing sentences: "For neither circumcision counts for anything, nor uncircumcision, but a new creation" (6:15). What is circumcision, but the making of external marks in a man's body, and what religious importance is there in that? The only thing that really matters is "new creation," that is, men and women made new people by the transforming power of God's Spirit. (The rabbis used the term "new creation" of a convert brought to the true knowledge of God.) May peace and mercy, he adds (6:16), be "upon all who walk by this rule"—all who live by this great principle; be "upon the Israel of God"—the Christian Church as the inheritor of the promises made to Abraham.

Then he flings a word of final defiance at his enemies. "Henceforth let no man trouble me; for I bear on my body the marks of Jesus" (6:17). These words have evoked much discussion. Nobody is in any doubt about what Paul has in mind; it is his scars, gotten in the service of Jesus. But why does he call them "stigmata," brand-marks, and why do they entitle him to cry defiance at his foes? In the ancient world, those devoted to the service of a deity often received brand-marks which not only indicated *ownership* but were also supposed to *protect* the bearer of them against assault. "On whomsoever the stigmata are placed," says Herodotus, "he gives himself to God and may not be touched." What Paul says here, therefore, is something like this: "It is futile to attack me. My scars proclaim that I am Jesus' servant and immune from harm."

With a prayer that grace—the wonderful kindness of Christ to sinners—may be with their spirit, and an affectionate "brethren," the Epistle of Christian Freedom comes to an end.

EPHESIANS

INTRODUCTION

Authorship

Were a vote taken to decide which is the greatest of Paul's letters, the verdict would probably go to Romans, but many would choose Ephesians—John Calvin, for example, who called it his favorite epistle, and Samuel Taylor Coleridge, who pronounced it one of the divinest compositions of man.

It comes, therefore, as something of a shock to some to learn that many interpreters of Ephesians, especially in Germany and the United States, refuse the letter to the one man in the Early Church apparently capable of writing it and attribute it to a disciple of Paul's—"a Paulinist," as the phrase goes. The most ingenious modern theory is that its author was none other than the ex-runaway slave Onesimus, who first gathered Paul's letters together and then wrote Ephesians to serve as an introduction to them. We must therefore, in loyalty to truth, face the question: Why has Paul's authorship come under suspicion, and is the doubt justified?

It is right and proper to start from the fact that the doubt is quite modern. From early in the second century everybody took the letter to be Paul's; Irenaeus cited it under Paul's name, and his predecessors undoubtedly shared his conviction; and a list of New Testament books deemed canonical in Rome about A.D. 180 (the so-called Muratorian Canon) attributed it to Paul. Not till the nineteenth century did anybody dream that the book was not Paul's own work.

On what grounds has the doubt been based?

First, it is alleged that the vocabulary and style are unlike Paul's. Ephesians contains eighty-two words not found in Paul's admittedly genuine letters. But this fact seems quite unimpressive when we learn that the shorter Colossians (usually accepted as Paul's) contains no less than fifty-six new words, and that the

in Philippians (indisputably Paul's)
 phesians. The doubters then bid us note
f Ephesians uses words like "body," "stew-
ery," which occur also in Colossians, he uses
different sense. When this is challenged, as it
sk us to observe the general style of Ephesians
, involved sentences which contrast strangely, they
he terse, explosive vigor of Paul's customary man-
e again, it is sufficient to answer that the explosive style
beh. controversial writing like Galatians, but is inappropriate
in a devotional writing like Ephesians; that the first chapter of
Colossians also contains long, involved sentences; and that a
writer of Paul's versatility was surely capable of both styles.

Such stylistic tests being admittedly imprecise, the doubters
next assure us that the *doctrine* of Ephesians is un-Pauline. Here
they fasten on such points in Ephesians as (1) that the Gentiles
have a share with the ancient people of God in the blessings of
the gospel; (2) that the role of the Church in God's dealings
with the world goes beyond anything found in Paul's earlier letters; and (3) that such a sentence as the one in 3:4, with its
claim to special insight by Paul, is impossible on Paul's lips. But,
surely, none of these things is incompatible with the real Paul.
Do they not all have parallels and anticipations in his earlier and
admittedly authentic epistles? And if in Ephesians they seem
more highly developed, is not this just what we might expect in
a letter written near the end of Paul's life, when his mind was
at its maturest? Who is likelier to have drawn out the deepest implications of earlier doctrines than the Apostle himself?

Finally, the doubters invoke the *literary links* between Colossians and Ephesians. More than one-third of the words and
phrases in Colossians reappear in Ephesians, and there are passages in Ephesians which seem to have been patterned on corresponding ones in Colossians. Here we are invited to detect the
copying hand of one of Paul's disciples. But the alleged copying
is done with such freedom and subtlety that other people draw
the quite opposite conclusion—in Paul's favor. Besides, they
add, if Ephesians was written soon after Colossians, would
not many phrases of the first letter be still running in his head?

At this point three considerations may be added to the case
for the defense:

To begin with, the point of the passage about Tychicus (6:21-

22) is not at all clear if the letter is not Paul's. This reference has all the marks of genuineness.

Second, the complete unanimity of the Early Church about Paul's authorship should be remembered.

Third, Ephesians is, by the consent even of the ones who doubt Pauline authorship, a work of high spiritual genius. If we say Paul did not write it, we must posit the existence in the Early Church of a "Great Unknown" who was Paul's spiritual equal. Was there such a man?

Clearly the burden of proof lies with those who deny Paul's authorship. Unless and until such conclusive proof is forthcoming, we may regard the letter as Paul's and we may believe (with tradition) that it was written during his imprisonment in Rome— written, indeed, soon after Colossians—and carried by Tychicus on the journey to Asia on which Onesimus accompanied him (Col. 4:7-9).

Destination and Purpose

But was Ephesians really addressed (as the title suggests) to the Christians in Ephesus? The title goes back to the second century, since it occurs in a papyrus manuscript coming from that period. But two facts in the letter itself give us pause: First, the omission of the words "in Ephesus" (1:1) by our three oldest and best manuscripts of the New Testament; and, second, the fact that the writer does not seem to know his readers personally (1:15 and 3:2), as Paul undoubtedly knew the Christians in Ephesus. What then? The solution is to regard Ephesians as a circular letter, or encyclical, sent to the Gentile churches in Asia. This view would explain not only the lack of the words "in Ephesus" but also the absence of personal greetings at the end. In the original letter Paul would have left a blank space in the address, and it would have been the duty of Tychicus (who carried the letter) to fill in the appropriate place name, as he visited the various churches. In this encyclical the Apostle, having just written Colossians, and with all the Gentile Christians of Asia in his mind, sets down for his readers his profoundest and maturest thoughts about the role of Christ and his Church in God's great purposes for men, his aim being to confirm them in their faith, widen their spiritual horizons, and draw them closer in their bonds of Christian unity and brotherhood.

The Message of Ephesians

The theme of Ephesians is the glory of the Church as *the society which embodies in history the eternal purpose of God made plain in Christ*. This emphasizes certain central ideas:

The Eternal Purpose. A divine intention runs through history. The ultimate reality is a Father, he has a purpose of love for all, and his will is for community. But the cosmos reveals a great rift—demonic powers marring the divine order, and sinful men at enmity with one another. Of himself, man cannot repair the rift; only God can, and he purposes to subdue all opposing powers—human and superhuman—to his will, and to create a great unity.

The Centrality of Christ. The gospel is the good news of God's unveiled secret. (This is what Paul means by his expression, "the mystery." The word signifies a secret plan in the divine mind which is now being disclosed to the world.) This unveiled secret is Christ, who is not merely the Messiah of the Jews but the Clue to history and the Meaning of the universe. God's purpose is embodied in Christ's Person and in the victory which he wrought by his dying, rising, and ascending; and that purpose is the reconciliation of all created things.

The Glory of the Church. The purpose of God is to be realized through the Church. The Church is the Body of Christ, the social organism which is to execute God's purpose in the world. The Eternal God wills fellowship; in that fellowship Jews and Gentiles are now included; and this process will go on till all who believe are reconciled to God in Christ.

Such is the doctrine of Ephesians, but it carries with it clear moral demands. These are set forth in the four great charges in the second half of the letter. Christians are summoned to promote the Church's unity, to renounce pagan ways, to build up Christian homes, and to put on the whole armor of God as they carry the battle with evil to the farthest frontiers of thought and action. To that end they are called to "live in the light," to "learn Christ," and to "walk in the Spirit."

No book of the New Testament is more relevant to our day and generation. It holds before Christian men and women the vision of the Church as the working Body of Christ, and of its mission to bind all nations in a brotherhood of worship and love. It says to men cowering behind their ideological iron curtains and living a kind of barbed-wire existence: Unite—or perish!

OUTLINE

Few of Paul's letters are easier to analyze than this one. It falls into two main sections, the first doctrinal, the second ethical, or practical. The theme of the first three chapters is God's eternal purpose for man, manifested in Christ and his Church; the theme of the last three chapters is the pattern of Christian life which ought to be lived by the members of Christ's Church. The following scheme of contents is that which is followed in the commentary:

Salutation. Ephesians 1:1-2

Doctrine. Ephesians 1:3—3:21

> Doxology (1:3-14)
> Prayer for His Readers' Enlightenment (1:15—2:10)
> The Reconciliation of Jew and Gentile in Christ (2:11-22)
> Paul's Commission to the Gentiles (3:1-13)
> Paul's Prayer for the Gentiles' Strengthening (3:14-21)

Ethics. Ephesians 4:1—6:20

> First Charge: to Promote the Church's Unity (4:1-16)
> Second Charge: to Break with Pagan Ways (4:17—5:20)
> Third Charge: to Build Christian Homes (5:21—6:9)
> Fourth Charge: to Put on the Armor of God (6:10-20)

Conclusion. Ephesians 6:21-24

COMMENTARY

SALUTATION

Ephesians 1:1-2

"Dear So-and-so" is the way we begin our letters. The ancients did it rather differently; for them, "A to B, greeting" was their usual formula, often followed by a prayer for the reader's health. Paul, of course, follows the conventional formula, but he often expands it in order to say something about himself or his gospel (see, for example, the discussion of Galatians 1:1-5). Here, however, his opening is very simple. He calls himself the "apostle," that is, the "special messenger" of Christ Jesus; his addressees are "the saints who are also faithful in Christ Jesus." Notice two points here. The first (already mentioned in the Introduction) is that the words "in Ephesus," familiar to us from the King James Version, do not occur in our oldest and best manuscripts, and can hardly be a part of the original writing. If, as we have suggested, Ephesians was originally a circular letter for the churches in Asia, Paul must have left a blank space here for Tychicus to fill in as he went among the churches. The other point is the meaning of the word "saints." By saints nowadays we mean virtuosos in goodness, or people who have been canonized by the Roman Catholic Church as great Christians. But the root meaning of the word is "set apart" to God's service, and when originally applied to Israel in the Old Testament (for example, in Ps. 148:14) it described them as "the dedicated people of God." The Christian Church, we know, took over the titles which had belonged to the old Israel, believing the Church to be the new and true Israel. "Saints" was one of these titles. In the New Testament it is a synonym for Christians as members of the new people of God, that is, of the Church of Christ. The emphasis falls on their commitment or dedication to God, rather than on their personal holiness, although of course they are called to grow day by day in the holiness for which Christ gives the pattern.

These "saints" are also "faithful in Christ Jesus." Here we have the first example in Ephesians of Paul's master phrase, "in Christ." Their faith is rooted in Christ—the Christ who is not only their personal Savior but also the Head of the new people of God, of which they are members. For them all, Paul prays "grace . . . and peace from God our Father and the Lord Jesus Christ." Notice how Christ stands with the Father on that side of reality which we call divine. "Grace," one of Paul's great words, signifies the unmerited love of God in Christ to sinners. "Peace" is that serenity of soul which comes to those who have been reconciled to God.

DOCTRINE

Ephesians 1:3—3:21

Doxology (1:3-14)

Into the splendid opening doxology Paul sweeps the various stages in God's great purpose to sum up all things in Christ: his election of us in eternity, his saving act through Christ in time, the inclusion of Jew and Gentile in the new divine Society, our sealing with the Holy Spirit, and the full fruition of salvation. In the very first verse of the doxology we meet a phrase, "in the heavenly places," which occurs five times in Ephesians and means "in the spiritual world."

All begins in the mind of "the God and Father of our Lord Jesus Christ" (1:3), the God who had revealed himself uniquely to Jesus as *Abba*, Father, and had raised him from the dead. In blessing us in Christ, God was executing a great purpose conceived in eternity. Willing "that we should be holy and blameless before him," God "chose us in him before the foundation of the world" (1:4). God's dealings with us are dealings of love. They began before time, and they had as their aim that we should be God's "sons through Jesus Christ" (1:5). To describe our sonship, Paul uses the figure of adoption. It serves to make clear that although Christ is Son by nature, we become sons only by grace. In the expression "to the praise of his glorious grace which he freely bestowed on us in the Beloved," the last two words are a Messianic title for Christ, in whom that grace was gloriously exhibited.

Let us pause to note the stress in these verses on the ideas of predestination and the grace of God working in us even before we turn to him. Paul believes in election—that God, as the supreme Disposer of events, saves men and marks them out for glory. This is a doctrine which sometimes, among extreme Calvinists, has been so expressed as to invite bitter criticism. In reply, three simple things may be said in defense of Paul's doctrine. First, whatever some Calvinists have taught, Paul did not teach the doctrine of "double predestination"; namely, that God has from all eternity elected a few to everlasting bliss, and predestined the majority to everlasting torment. Second, when Paul speaks of predestination, he speaks as a saved man rather than as a systematic theologian. A man who has experienced God's grace cannot regard it as an accidental affair; he comes to feel that, without any will or act of his own, God has marked him out for salvation. It is only when we try to turn this experience into a theological dogma that we run into ultimate mystery and raise insoluble problems. Third, firmly as Paul holds to the idea of election, he no less firmly believes in human responsibility, and recognizes that a man may fall from the place in grace to which God has elected him. Basically, the doctrine of election is rooted in the conviction that we do not just happen to exist, that our lives have their roots in eternity, that our salvation begins in the mind of the Eternal God, and that it is brought to realization in Christ, the divinely sent Savior of men.

To this realization Paul now turns (1:7). God's eternal purpose was fulfilled when Christ came and redeemed us from our sins. "In him we have redemption through his blood, the forgiveness of our trespasses" (see Col. 1:14). "Redemption" denoted originally the ransoming of a slave from bondage by the payment of a sum of money. Later it came to have the more general meaning of "deliverance," with the idea of price well in the background. The Greek Old Testament used the word to describe God's "deliverance" of Israel from Egyptian bondage. Paul uses it of God's deliverance of his people from sin and death—a deliverance effected through the blood of Christ; that is, through Christ's atoning death, which was "according to the riches of his grace which he lavished upon us" (1:8). How often Paul returns to the wonderful kindness of God in Christ to us undeserving men!

But God has not stopped at forgiving us; he has given us "wisdom and insight" into "the mystery of his will" (1:9). "Mystery" here means the secret purpose of God in his dealings with men, a secret that is now being disclosed in the gospel. Hitherto, Paul would say, God's will—his plan for the world—had remained a riddle; now in Christ the riddle is being made plain. In him God's purpose is unveiled, and is seen to be nothing less than his intention "for the fullness of time, to unite all things in him," be they "things in heaven" or "things on earth" (1:10). The phrase "the fullness of time" means that God has acted at the time when he saw all things to be ready. And now the full range, the cosmic scope, of his saving design is made clear. God plans to *unite*—to gather up, bring into focus—everything he has made, in Christ. Christ is to be the principle of unity. Where disorder had reigned, there is to be order; where conflict, concord—God's order, God's concord.

The first act in this great drama has now been played, as Paul goes on to say (1:11-14). It is the union of Jews and Gentiles in the Church of Christ. This is in accordance with God's sovereign purpose. "We who first hoped in Christ" (1:12) must mean Jewish Christians who had anticipated the Gentiles in putting their hope in Christ. But the Greek might also mean, "we who before hoped in the Messiah." The reference would then be to the Jewish people with their Messianic hope. Paul next turns to address the Gentiles (1:13). They, too, share in Christ, for they have accepted "the word of truth" (the Christian revelation, we would say), further defined as "the gospel of your salvation." Furthermore, they have been "sealed with the promised Holy Spirit, which is the guarantee of our inheritance until we acquire possession of it" (1:13-14). To "seal" was to put a proprietary mark on something. So, by the gift of the Holy Spirit at baptism, God marks out the believer in Christ as his own property. For the epithet "promised" see Luke 24:49, where Christ tells the disciples, "Behold, I send the promise of my Father upon you." Whenever a convert becomes conscious of "the life of God in the soul of man" (which is what the Holy Spirit means), that promise is fulfilled again, as it had first been spectacularly fulfilled on the Day of Pentecost (Acts 2). The Holy Spirit is called the "guarantee" of our heavenly inheritance. The Greek word rendered "guarantee" was originally a commercial term meaning a "down payment" or "first installment," given in pledge that the whole sum would be paid later. In the same way our experience of the Holy Spirit in our hearts is God's advance guarantee of his will and intention to pay in full, when he consummates our salvation in the bliss of heaven. Then we shall enjoy "all those blessed things that God has prepared for them that love him."

Prayer for His Readers' Enlightenment (1:15—2:10)

Paul's thanksgiving for the faith and love of the "Ephesians" passes quickly into a prayer that God will enable them to realize the glories to which he has called them and the greatness of the power he has put at their disposal. It is the power which took Christ out of the grave and made him Lord of the universe and Head of the Church.

When one lives in the midst of a pagan world, as Paul did, he undoubtedly soon learns to thank God for the faith and love of the Christian men and women around him (1:15). By "faith" Paul means faith in the Lord Jesus. It is directed not to a proposition but to a person, and it is essentially trust in Christ as the divine Son of God, the saving revelation of the unseen Father. Similarly, "love" is not sentimentality or emotionalism of any kind, but "caring"—caring for other people because God has "cared" for us by giving us Christ. (Many ancient manuscripts omit the word "love" in verse 15, but the Revised Standard Version is probably right in retaining it, as in Colossians 1:4.)

Verse 17 introduces the actual prayer. It is addressed to "the God of our Lord Jesus Christ, the Father of glory," the last phrase suggesting One whom we may approach with the confidence of little children yet who, as the Source of all perfection, is infinitely adorable. Paul prays that God will give them "a spirit of wisdom and of revelation in the knowledge of him." By "knowledge" is meant no arid and scholastic dogma, but personal communion with God based on trust and obedience. As they grow in that saving knowledge, he asks that "the eyes of their hearts" may be "enlightened" (1:18). In the Bible the heart is the seat not so much of the emotions as of the understanding, so that this is a prayer that Paul's readers may have their spiritual wits sharpened to understand three things: "the hope to which he has called you"—the blessed hope of everlasting life; "the riches of his glorious inheritance in the saints"—the glory and wonder of that life among the heavenly beings; and "the immeasurable greatness of his power in us who believe"—that is, the presence in us even now of God's power to help us realize this life (1:18-19).

On this power Paul now enlarges. It is power "according to the working of his great might which he accomplished in Christ when he raised him from the dead and made him sit at his right hand in the heavenly places" (1:19-20). The power, Paul says, which is available for you now in your Christian living is the same power which took Christ out of the grave and put him on the throne of the universe. For this is where Christ is now: "far above all rule and authority and power and dominion, and above every name that is named, not only in this age but also in that which is to come" (1:21). Was the doctrine of the regnant Christ ever phrased more impressively? Paul and his contemporaries conceived of the unseen world as peopled by all sorts of "discarnate intelligences," some good, some evil. "Whatever angelic beings there may be," he says in effect, "Christ has outsoared them all"; and he rounds off his catalogue of these powers with a reference to "every name that is named"; that is, every conceivable dignity that may exist now or at any future time. How important and necessary is the Christian conviction not merely that Christ is alive now but that he sits with his Father on the throne of the universe!

This is precisely the point that Paul underscores in the next verse (22), where God "has put all things under his feet." Here Paul applies the words of Psalm 8:6 to Christ. But with the next phrase he turns to Christ's headship over the Church. God, he says, has made Christ "head over all things for the church, which is his body, the fullness of him who fills all in all" (1:22-23). Of all Paul's doctrines none has been more fruitful than this concept of the Church as the Body of Christ. The Hebrew idea of "corporate personality," including the sense of solidarity of the group and of the involvement of each member in the others, no doubt made possible the metaphor in the first instance, if it is, indeed, only a metaphor and not something more—something that signals at reality. Probably the title, the "Body," was born in the context of the sacrament of the Lord's Supper, where Christians expressed their oneness by eating the one loaf which symbolized Christ's body (see I Cor. 10:16-17). In any case, it sets forth the Church as a living organism, with the ascended Christ as its controlling Head, called to do his work in the world, as once his own body of flesh and blood had done it. To this day, and as long as the world lasts, this will be the essential idea of the Church—an organism truly responsive to the impulses of the mind and heart of Christ, an organism sacrificially expendable in the carrying out of his great and gracious purposes.

But a difficult point stands right at the close of the chapter.

In what sense is the Church, as Christ's Body, "the fullness of him who fills all in all"? We can see how the Church, as pervaded by Christ's life, can be called "his fullness." But in view of the Greek construction here, the phrase, "who fills all in all," should probably be rendered: "who is all in all being filled." For Paul, Christ is a corporate personality in whom the Church lives and grows (see 2:21). There is a sense in which Christ cannot be said to be complete until this growing is ended. So the phrase will mean: "the totality of him [Christ] who is everywhere and in all respects growing complete." When, in God's providence, this comes to pass, "the Christ that is to be" will be a blessed reality.

The main idea in this paragraph in 2:1-10 is that the Gentiles have been raised from the death of sin to new life by the gift of God in Christ. But in the course of the discussion many of Paul's characteristic doctrines emerge: the universality of sin, the power of the Devil in human affairs, the wrath of God, justification by faith, and the place of good works in the Christian's life.

In the opening phrase, "And you he made alive," there is no real break with the preceding chapter. The Revised Standard Version, for clarity's sake, sets the main verb at the beginning, though in the Greek it does not appear till verse 5. For the thought see the similar section in Colossians 2:13. Gentile sin is fully discussed in Romans 1:18-32. In Ephesians Paul is content to affirm that the Gentiles were dead in their sins and under the Devil's power. The Devil, who is called "the prince of the power of the air," is said to be "now at work in the sons of disobedience," that is, in men who have departed from God's ways. With his contemporaries Paul held that the Devil and his minions inhabited the upper air, whence they exerted a malign influence on men. Nowadays our scientists who send rockets into outer space do not reckon on their having to pass through a "demonic belt" on the way. Paul's cosmology is as outmoded as many of our present scientific theories will be in a hundred years. But this is not to say that the Devil does not exist: indeed, there is no reason why the cosmos should not contain spirits higher than man, who have made evil their good, and whose activities are co-ordinated by a master strategist. The permanent value of Paul's words here is their suggestion of the mysterious nature of evil. We, too, are tempted to the doing of evil deeds by dark forces which we can neither fathom nor control.

But the Gentiles were not the only people dead in sin. "We

all once lived in the passions of our flesh" (2:3), says Paul, setting the Jews on a level with the Gentiles. "Flesh" is the material side of our nature, and it is not necessarily bad. But, since sin has infected it, the flesh normally signifies for Paul our fallen human nature—human nature as apostate from God—and to trust in the flesh is to live God-lessly, in sinful self-reliance. Such a way of life inevitably made us "children of wrath, like the rest of mankind." We deserved God's holy displeasure.

What does Paul mean by "the wrath of God"? Many people react against the phrase, which occurs some sixteen times in Paul's writings. They hold that anger is foreign to God's nature and interpret it in terms of some impersonal doctrine of retribution—the inevitable operation of cause and effect in a moral world. But the Bible does not do this. For the Old Testament prophets the divine wrath is a personal activity; and, though Jesus taught us that God is a loving Father, he found the divine reaction to sin an awful reality. So does Paul. By the wrath of God he means God's holy displeasure at sin—the eternal reaction against evil without which God would not be the Moral Governor of the world—a reaction operative at the present time (Rom. 1:18) and destined to come to climax at the Last Judgment. We cannot, then, discard the doctrine; but we can remember two things. First, God's wrath cannot be the same as sinful man's. We must not picture God as an irascible man who suddenly loses his temper and casts his love aside. Rather should we think of a really good man's righteous indignation in the presence of stark evil, and then multiply it by infinity. Second, only a sentimental theology will find God's wrath incompatible with his love. The opposite of love is hate, not wrath. We should conceive wrath as the obverse of God's love, "the adverse wind," the antagonism of his holy love to all that is evil.

"But God," begins the next section (2:4-5). Man's extremity is God's opportunity. Having diagnosed our spiritual disease, Paul now describes God's remedy. It is a remedy which originates in the divine love—"out of the great love with which he loved us," is directed to our deadness in sin, and issues in heavenly life with Christ.

Note the three phrases: "made us alive," "raised us up," "made us sit" (2:5-6). In the Greek the verbs are all compounded with the same preposition, which means "together with," and they show that these are shared experiences, shared with Christ and shared with our fellow Christians. "God . . . made us alive together with Christ" (2:4-5). Any man who has passed suddenly from the death of sin to new life with Christ will know what these words mean. But Paul goes further: "God . . . made us sit with him in the heavenly places in Christ Jesus" (2:4-6). This is no "pie in the sky" religion, concerned only with future benefits; it is a doctrine of heaven now, heaven in the present tense, heaven here on earth. Does this language seem far too seraphic for most of us? Then it shows how far we fall short of the New Testament experience. If our trust in Christ were stronger, if we really let the Holy Spirit have his way with us, we would not find such language unreal. And God has done all this, Paul says, in order that he may show his grace and goodness to us "in the coming ages," that is, in all eternity (2:7).

Into his discussion of the new life Paul had inserted a parenthesis—"by grace you have been saved" (2:5). Now he repeats it in an amplified form: "by grace you have been saved through faith; and this is not your own doing, it is the gift of God—not because of works, lest any man should boast" (2:8-9). The "man" is reminiscent of the Pharisee in Christ's parable who paraded his good works before God (Luke 18:9-14). But the whole passage is so full of Paul's teaching about justification that it must be discussed.

Paul taught that no man can put himself right with God by his own achievements, however meritorious. Our salvation begins in the pure, undeserved goodness of God (which is what "grace" means), and all that is needed of us in return is our willingness to accept the offer of God's grace in Christ. The name for this response of ours is "faith," which is trust and obedience. This truth we find hard to learn. By misguided efforts of our own we frustrate God's good will to help us, like the drowning man who refuses to trust himself wholly to his rescuer and by his struggles only hampers attempts at rescue. We need to learn to commit ourselves unreservedly to God's grace in Christ.

This is the heart of Paul's doctrine, but he expresses it in law-court language which puzzles many people. Yet the essence of it is very simple and represents the teaching of our Lord himself no less than of his Apostle. Thus the parable of the Prodigal Son teaches that God is a God of grace who justifies (forgives) the ungodly who come to him in penitence. On man's side, the wrong approach to God is that of the Pharisee who boasted to

God of his good works; whereas the right approach is that of the publican, who, owning his own unworthiness, was content to cast himself on God's mercy (Luke 18:9-14). For there is only one way into the kingdom of God, which is the realm of salvation: "Whoever does not receive the kingdom of God like a child [receiving a present from his father] shall not enter it" (Mark 10:15).

We may be grateful that Paul added verse 10, for it delivers him from the charge, often made against him, that he had no use for good works. Paul insisted on the need for good works as much as anyone else, but—and this is the point—as the *outcome* and not the *cause* of man's salvation. Salvation is by grace "for good works" (2:10). Goodness for Paul is "grace goodness," the fine flowering of grace in a man's conduct; and the good works of a Christian are done, not in order to procure God's grace and favor, but *because* as a Christian he has already experienced them. The good works are, as Paul says here, "the end product," which God had in view when he began his gracious dealings with the man.

The Reconciliation of Jew and Gentile in Christ (2:11-22)

Paul now returns to his main theme, God's great purpose of unity in Christ. This purpose, he says, may now be seen to be taking shape in the Church, where the two hostile sections of humanity, Jews and Gentiles, are worshiping in one fellowship.

He begins by reminding the Gentiles that formerly they ranked, with respect to God's purposes, as complete outsiders (2:11-12). Jew and Gentile, circumcision and uncircumcision—these were the current titles, titles based on external distinctions of race and an artificial mark in the flesh. But it was the spiritual disabilities of the Gentiles that really mattered. They were "separated from Christ," which is the opposite of all it means to be "in Christ." What disadvantages did this bring? There were four: no knowledge of the one true God; no membership in his divine Society; no promise of future blessing; no hope of a life beyond death. Only by an effort of the historical imagination can one picture their spiritual deprivation: no certainty that there is a Father behind all things, but only a vague belief in "gods many and lords many"; no comforting sense of belonging to God's people; no promises of the divine will to shape the course of history to a good and gracious end; no hope beyond death of a Father's house with "many rooms" (John 14:2).

From all these blessings the Gentiles had been shut out. "But now in Christ Jesus," says Paul (2:13), the distance between the privileged and the unprivileged has been done away—by the Cross. "You who once were far off have been brought near in the blood of Christ." Back of this lies Isaiah 57:19:

"Peace, peace, to the far and to the near, says the LORD;
   and I will heal him."

Once "far" from God, the Gentiles have been brought near, and the means is Christ's atoning death—truly an At-one-ment! On Calvary Christ has reconciled Jew and Gentile with each other and with God. To the developing of this thought Paul now turns.

Peace? Yes, Paul says, taking the word from Isaiah 57:19, Jesus is "our peace" (2:14), the reconciler between Jew and Gentile, for he has "made us both one, and has broken down the dividing wall of hostility." In the Temple area at Jerusalem stood a stone fence, some five feet high, separating the Court of the Gentiles from the inner precincts. Notices on this fence (one of which was discovered in 1871) warned the intruding Gentile that if he crossed it, he was liable to death. That fence was a symbol of the hostility between Jew and Gentile. But all that it symbolized, Paul says, Christ has done away. How? By "abolishing in his flesh the law of commandments and ordinances" (2:15). This is the Jewish Law with its hundred and one rules and regulations, the whole effect of which was to maintain the separateness of the Jewish people and make their holy exclusiveness distasteful to the Gentiles. It was "in his flesh"— through his human life and death—that Christ did this. Thus, by abolishing the Law in his death, he abolished that which separated Jew and Gentile.

Not only so, but "he came and preached peace to you who were far off and peace to those who were near" (2:17). The "far off" folk are the Gentiles, the "near" ones the Jews. Paul is thinking here of the ministry of the regnant Christ through his Apostles, who carry his message of reconciliation to all men. And the blessed issue of all this is that "through him [Christ] we both [Jews and Gentiles] have access . . . to the Father"—admission to his Presence. This access is "in one Spirit"—the Holy Spirit who creates fellowship and unity wherever he does his special work. No verse in the New Testament better expresses what has been called "the Trinity of experience."

Then Paul draws his conclusions (2:19-22). The Gentiles are "no longer strangers and sojourners." The last word means in Greek a "resident alien" who, though possessing certain privileges, has no citizen rights. On the contrary, the Gentiles are "fellow citizens with the saints," fully enfranchised members of God's people and members of God's family.

"The household of God" is Paul's actual phrase here, and it allows him to change his metaphor from a *body* to a *building*. The Church of Christ, he now says, is a spiritual temple. Its foundation consists of "the apostles and prophets," meaning Christian prophets, not the seers of the Old Covenant. Christ himself is its "cornerstone," the stone forming the angle of a pediment or gable and so completing the entire building. In Christ "the whole structure is joined together and grows into a holy temple in the Lord" (2:21). This is no edifice of stone and lime but a spiritual house whose stones are living men and women in whom God dwells by his Spirit (2:22); and into this spiritual temple the Gentiles are being built.

Paul's Commission to the Gentiles (3:1-13)

It is a habit of Paul's to "go off at a word," as here. "I, Paul, a prisoner for Christ Jesus on behalf of you Gentiles," he begins (3:1), and off he goes at the word "Gentiles." Not until verse 14 does the verb of the sentence appear. In the clause, "assuming that you have heard of the stewardship of God's grace that was given to me," notice should be taken of the expression, "you have heard." If Paul had been writing only to the Ephesians, he would hardly have said this. "May I take it," is his meaning, "that you have heard how the gracious God gave me a special commission to you and revealed to me his secret?" The secret or "mystery" is God's world-purpose in the Incarnation, especially here as it affects the Gentiles. "As I have written briefly," says Paul, and adds: "When you read this you can perceive my insight into the mystery of Christ" (3:3-4). The writing referred to must be the previous paragraph. "I have said enough tiere," he declares, "to let you see that I have some knowledge of the secret of Christ." This secret, not disclosed to past generations, "has now been revealed to his holy apostles and prophets by the Spirit" (3:5). Those who doubt Paul's authorship of this letter (see the Introduction) think that Paul would hardly have called the Apostles "holy." But "holy" surely means "dedicated" and describes status rather than personal sanctity. Why should Paul not have so spoken? The "prophets," as in 2:20, must be the Christian prophets. Paul's words about the secret remind us of what Jesus said to his disciples about the Kingdom of God as a present reality: "Blessed are the eyes which see what you see! For I tell you that many prophets and kings desired to see what you see, and did not see it, and to hear what you hear, and did not hear it" (Luke 10:23-24). Then (3:6) comes the content of the secret: it is that the Gentiles are to be partakers with the Jews in the same inheritance, members of the same Body, and sharers in the same high destiny in Christ. The wonder of their privilege appears in Paul's threefold phrase: co-heirs, co-members, co-sharers.

Paul now (3:7) describes his call to the ministry of this gospel. As ever, he throws all the stress on the sheer grace of God, straining the very grammar to express his own unworthiness. "The very least of all the saints" (3:8) would be literally translated "the leaster of all the saints," the superlative form of the adjective being joined with a comparative termination. But, then, are not God's best servants always most conscious of their own imperfections? Two tasks the grace of God laid upon him. The first was missionary—"to preach to the Gentiles the unsearchable riches of Christ." The adjective, found also in Romans 11:33, suggests the inexplorable wealth of the fact of Christ. Christ is like a vast treasure house, in which a man may wander endlessly without exhausting its riches.

The second task laid on him was theological—"to make all men see what is the plan of the mystery hidden for ages in God who created all things" (3:9). This sentence views the gospel as a "mystery hidden," that is, a secret purpose of God as old as creation, but only now being revealed in Christ. A military illustration may help. In wartime the Supreme Command makes a plan and labels it "top secret." Until battle is joined it is hidden. Then the reasons for all the moves and maneuvers become clear. Thus it has been with God's plan of salvation. All creation and history exist with Christ in view.

From this Paul moves to the no less majestic thought that God's wisdom in redemption is an object of contemplation to the spirit-rulers of the universe: "that through the church the manifold wisdom of God might now be made known to the principalities and powers in the heavenly places" (3:10). Here the background to Paul's thinking is unmistakably first-century. We do not nowadays think of the universe as a series of spheres, between the earth and the highest heaven, peopled by spirit-beings. Nevertheless the sublimity of Paul's conception is arresting. His point is that the existence of Christ's Church, uniting hostile sections of mankind in one Body, is a plain proof, not to be ignored by whatever superhuman beings the universe may contain, that God is gathering up all creation in Christ. A truly wonderful idea of the Church! In all the wide universe nothing is so significant as God's redemption of men in Christ. When Goethe was asked in his old age to what conclusion he had come after a lifetime spent in thinking, he replied: "That the world exists for spiritual ends." Paul shares this conclusion, but adds that these ends are being realized in the Church. Here, then, we encounter not only the Cosmic Christ (as in Colossians) but the cosmos-witnessing Church. Angels, said Peter (I Peter 1:12), long to peer into the gospel. It is the Church's role, says Paul, to proclaim to all "discarnate intelligences" the "many-splendored wisdom of God" exhibited in the story of our redemption.

"This was according to the eternal purpose which he has realized in Christ Jesus our Lord" (3:11). "Eternal purpose" is literally "purpose of the ages." This divine purpose has come to fruition in Christ, who is "our Lord, in whom we have boldness and confidence of access through our faith in him" (3:11-12). The Lord, who is the support and stay of our Christian faith, is also the Crown of the world's development.

The long parenthesis, replete with soaring insights and splendors of expression, ends with a reference to Paul's bonds (3:13). "No despairing, my friends," he says in effect; "the sufferings of Christ's messengers are a call to courage, not a cause for losing heart." When a martyr testifies against all tyrants to his faith in Christ, the gospel speeds on and triumphs, and skeptics are moved to admiration.

Paul's Prayer for the Gentiles' Strengthening (3:14-21)

Now at last Paul falls on his knees and his prayer matches his parenthesis in its sublimity. The usual posture in prayer was standing (Mark 11:25; Luke 18:11, 13); the fact that Paul bows his knees (3:14) suggests the earnestness of his prayer. It is addressed to "the Father, from whom every family in heaven and on earth is named" (3:14-15). The Greek here has a play on words hardly reproducible in English, for the word translated "family" is etymologically derived from the word translated "Father." "Is named" means "derives its name and nature." God, Paul says, is the Author of all imaginable fatherhood. So far from being a mere metaphor, his Fatherhood is the reality of which the human relationship is only a reflection; and whatever is meant by family relationships, on earth or in heaven, gains all the richness of its meaning from his Fatherhood.

Then follow the three petitions of the prayer. First, he prays that God through his grace may grant them to be "strengthened with might through his Spirit in the inner man" (3:16). The Holy Spirit in the New Testament is essentially the divine Dynamic of the new life, whose sphere of working is "the inner man" (see II Cor. 4:16); that is, man's higher nature, his reason, conscience, and will.

The second petition is "that Christ may dwell in your hearts through faith" (3:17). From the standpoint of Christian experience this is another form of the first petition, since it is through the Holy Spirit that the living Christ indwells a man's heart. The understanding of these words, moreover, is a matter of Christian experience rather than of exegesis. From the Day of Pentecost until today there have never been lacking men and women to tell how "the Christ of the story" has become "the Christ of the heart." This abiding presence of Christ is the Father's gift and is to be appropriated "through faith."

The third petition is for moral stability—that they may be "rooted and grounded in love" (3:17). One of the failings of Paul's Greek churches was that they set too much store by knowledge. Paul does not disparage true knowledge, but he never tires of insisting on the primacy of love. This is the key to unlock the deep things of the One whose nature is love. It will enable them, he goes on to say in verse 18, to "comprehend with all the saints what is the breadth and length and height and depth." There he stops short, without telling us to what these four dimensions apply. Beyond doubt, he means "the love of Christ," next mentioned in the text. But before it is discussed, notice should be taken of the phrase "with all the saints." What Paul implies here is that the secrets of the Faith are disclosed, not to solitary Christians, but to those who love the company of God's people and the common worship of the saints. Even so, in our time, we have been learning anew that all the best theology is written against the background of the believing and worshiping Church. In such a context Christians come to know best "the love of Christ which surpasses knowledge" (3:19). Paul means "Christ's love for us," which "none but his loved ones know." Yet it always remains too great to be fully known. This is one possible meaning of "surpasses knowledge." But possible, too, is the meaning that love is a greater thing than knowledge (I Cor. 13:2). The final issue of all that Paul prays for his readers is that they "may be filled with all the fullness of God," that they may embody in their corporate life the full content of the divine nature. Write "us" for "me" in the hymn "Breathe on Me, Breath of God," and its four stanzas make an excellent commentary on what Paul wills God to do for his readers.

It is Paul's habit to round off the great divisions in his letters with an ascription or a doxology (see Rom. 8, 11, and 15). So he does now. The boldness of the prayer he has just offered is warranted by the inconceivable greatness of God's power, and the fact that it is actually at work in human lives. "Now to him who by the power at work within us is able to do far more abundantly than all that we ask or think," he says (3:20), again summoning us to "think bigly" of God. But why the double phrase "in the church and in Christ Jesus" (3:21) in the ascription of glory? Because Christ and his Church are complementary parts in one organism—Head and Body—and together form the sphere in which God's power is shown forth. The whole doxology provides a splendid conclusion to the first part of the letter, reminding us that we do not realize a fraction of the adventurous possibilities of our Christian life or the blessings God has in store for us.

ETHICS
Ephesians 4:1—6:20

First Charge: to Promote the Church's Unity (4:1-16)

From doctrine to ethics. Having expounded God's great purpose for the world in Christ and the Church, Paul now turns, in chapters 4 through 6, to tell his readers how they ought to live as members of the Church, and the letter changes into a series of charges or exhortations.

"I therefore, a prisoner for the Lord, beg you to lead a life worthy of the calling to which you have been called" (4:1). This is the principle of *noblesse oblige,* a favorite one with Paul. Spiritual rank imposes moral obligations. The day-to-day behavior of the saints must match their status, for are they not members of Christ's Body, the Church, and called to share their Savior's glorious destiny? Therefore their conduct must manifest the Christlike qualities of humility and forbearance (4:2)—virtues never highly esteemed in the great pagan world before Christ came. Along with them must go an eagerness to "maintain the unity of the Spirit in the bond of peace" (4:3). It is the unity that the Holy Spirit creates which Paul has in mind, not mere similarity of outlook among people. Its "bond" or link is "peace."

Having appealed for unity, Paul now declares the religious basis on which this unity rests. Seven times he repeats the word "one," each time attaching to it a different noun. The result is a sevenfold battle cry of Christian unity. Note how this foundation for unity begins in the unity of the Church, goes on to the unity of Christ, and culminates in the unity of God:

"One body . . . one Spirit . . . one hope"—that is, one holy Fellowship, one life-giving Spirit informing it, and one goal on which its hope is set.

"One Lord, one faith, one baptism"—that is, one Savior to be worshiped and adored; one pledge or confession of trust in him; one rite of initiation into his Fellowship.

"One God and Father of us all, who is above all and through all and in all"—that is, the divine Father and Author of all in the threefoldness of his unity—transcendent, omnipresent, immanent. (For a simpler formula in an earlier letter see I Corinthians 8:6.)

A passage like this surely speaks to us today, concerned as we are for the Church's unity and all too aware of our "unhappy divisions." Yet when we worry, as we should, about our disunity, let us not forget the things on which Christians all over the world are united. All Christians of all races worship the same God and Father. All confess Christ as Savior and Lord. All share the same hope of salvation. All avow the primacy of the law of love. And, whatever form their worship takes, one Spirit is vouchsafed to all who meet in the name of Christ. The troubles begin when we reach the "bodily" marks of unity—"one body," "one baptism," and creedal expressions of "one faith"—not to mention the doctrine of the ministry, apostolic succession, and the question whether episcopacy is of the essential nature of the Church. Here are the issues to which we must address ourselves in that Christian charity and humility to which Paul so often calls us.

The theme of verses 7-16 is diversity in unity. All the members of Christ's Body have different offices, but each in its own way contributes to the Church's destined unity.

The first sentence (4:7) states the theme. Each Christian has his particular gift of grace from Christ. (Is there not here a word of encouragement for the Christian who may imagine there is nothing he can do?) Then Paul quotes Scripture (Ps. 68:18) to clinch his point:

> "When he ascended on high he led a host of captives, and he gave gifts to men" (4:8).

He applies these ancient words to Christ. When the Psalmist spoke of captives, he was picturing God as a conqueror marching up to the gates of a fallen city and taking tribute from the vanquished. Paul is thinking of Christ's victory over the demonic powers achieved on the cross (see Col. 2:15) and of the gifts of the Spirit which the risen and ascended Lord gave to his people.

In quoting Psalm 68:18, Paul changes a statement made about God *"receiving* gifts *among* men" to "he *gave* gifts *to* men." Paul was not the first to make these changes in the Psalm and to reapply it. There is a rabbinical Targum which applies the passage to Moses and reads: "He gave gifts to men."

Here (4:9-10) Paul pauses to comment on the words of the Psalm just quoted. Consider, he says, the words "He ascended." Obviously they imply Christ's previous descent "into the lower parts of the earth." Where is this? Some take it to refer to "the lower earth," this world below, in which case Paul is thinking of the Incarnation. But it is perhaps likelier that the reference is to the underworld, that is, to Hades (see I Peter 3:19). He does not stay to discuss this descent but goes on: "He who descended is he who also ascended far above all the heavens, that he might fill all things" (4:10). His point is that Christ has compassed the universe, from its depths to its heights, in order to pervade the whole of it with his Being.

With verse 11 Paul comes back to his main theme—the varying gifts of the exalted Christ to men. As God gave Christ to be the Church's Head, so Christ has given ministers to the Church to serve it in various ways. Some he made "apostles" like the Twelve and Paul and Barnabas; some, "prophets," men with a special gift for preaching (see Acts 11:27-28; 15:32; and I Cor. 14:3). Others he made "evangelists," missioners to the unconverted; and others, "pastors and teachers," settled ministers in local churches.

These gifts he made for a specific purpose: "for the equipment of the saints, for the work of ministry, for building up the body of Christ" (4:12). The sentence makes better sense if the comma after "saints" is removed. The sense, then, is that Christ gave these gifts in order to equip his people for the work of serving. And this equipment of his saints for service has for its great end, the building up of Christ's Body. The metaphors are mixed, no doubt. But what matter? The great aim of the Christian ministry is grandly stated.

What is the goal of all this upbuilding? It is "the unity of the faith and of the knowledge of the Son of God" (4:13). A common loyalty to the Savior, with lives which are lived by faith in the Son of God who loved them (Gal. 2:20)—this is the supreme end in view. When this comes to pass, the Church will have attained "mature manhood," and "the measure of the stature of the fullness of Christ." Paul sees the perfect Church not as a collection of perfected saints but as one full-grown man, or humanity, fully expressing what Christ is. The Church is viewed, not as so many individuals pressing on to perfection, but as a single organism growing to its full strength and becoming fit for the purpose which God intended for it.

If this great purpose is to be fulfilled, it is incumbent on the Church's members not to behave like immature children, or to veer about like ships in a gale, or to be led astray by clever deceivers (4:14). The right way is, by maintaining "the truth in love" to "grow up in every way into him who is the head" (4:15). It is a fine thing to speak the truth in love, as the Revised Standard Version translates here; but Paul's Greek asks for more than truth on the lips only. "Living by the truth"—that is, by the Christian revelation, and missing no chance of maintaining it in a spirit of Christian love—is what he means. This is the way for the Body to grow up into its Head.

The last verse of the charge, using anatomical language, pictures the Church as a social organism in which each member contributes to the growth of the whole by receiving and passing on the life drawn from Christ, the Head (see Col. 2:19). The anatomical theory is that of Paul's day (did Paul get it from Dr. Luke?). The ancient physiologists took the cohesion of the body to be due, not only to the contact of one part with another, but also to the nerves and ligaments which, like cords, bind the different parts together. But the secret of the Church's successful growing does not depend on anatomy but on "each part . . . working properly" and on its upbuilding itself "in love." Every Christian congregation can find food for thought here.

Second Charge: to Break with Pagan Ways (4:17—5:20)

Paul's second charge calls for a clean break with the old bad ways of paganism. The life of the Gentiles, which had once been theirs, is one of spiritual "futility" with "vanity of vanities" written all over it (4:17). Its marks are inward darkness and alienation from the true life God intended for men, founded as it is on "ignorance" and insensibility. So calloused in heart do they become that they give way to "licentiousness" in their greed "to practice every kind of uncleanness" (4:19). The word translated by "greedy" literally means "the desire to have more," and so expresses that ruthless self-assertion which tramples on the rights of others in order to satisfy its own impulses.

For another dark picture of pagan wickedness see Romans 1:18-32. Someone may well ask, Does not Paul put too much lampblack into his painting of the pagan world? Let us answer this question with another one: If Paul were writing today, would his picture of those who live the pagan life be much rosier? Some cultured humanists of our day who repudiate the Christian faith undoubtedly lead morally respectable lives; but not all. A goodly number of them dislike Christianity not so much for intellectual as for moral reasons, namely, because it insists on purity and chastity. In any case, no clear-sighted observer of our human situation can deny that when men and women reject the blessings and sanctions of Christianity, they relapse into ways of living not unlike Paul's Gentiles. Who will dare to say that "the world" today (which is the equivalent of "the Gentiles" in our letter) is not full of drunkenness, gambling, sexual vice, and that ruthless self-assertion which cares nothing for its neighbor's rights?

"You did not so learn Christ!" says Paul to his readers (4:20). (This is an understatement or, as the grammarians call it, litotes.) "Assuming that you have heard about him and were taught in him, as the truth is in Jesus" (4:21). Note the "in him," implying that their Christian instruction had come to them in living fellowship with Christ. For to "learn Christ" is not merely to master his story in the Gospels, or to pattern one's life on his teachings, but to find new life and power and hope in communion with him. But what does "as the truth is in Jesus" mean? "Truth" must signify, as it does so often in John, knowledge of divine reality; as the human name "Jesus" must allude to the historic person. The final truth of God, Paul is saying, is embodied in the Jesus of history.

"Put off your old nature . . . and put on the new nature" (4:22-24). The metaphors come from putting clothing on and off, and the tenses of the verbs in the Greek refer to a change which is to be made once for all. The "old nature" is the old Christ-less self which, Paul says, is in process of decaying through the passions that taint and warp a man's life. The cure for this is renewal "in the spirit [disposition] of your minds," the phrase implying that a true conversion will change a man's mental as well as his moral habits.

In the closing paragraph of this chapter Paul singles out six sins for condemnation and calls for the corresponding virtues.

First, quoting Zechariah 8:16, he insists on the duty of truthfulness as something we owe to the Christian society to which we belong. He continues, quoting Psalm 4:4: "Be angry but do not sin" (4:26). There is a place in the Christian life for righteous indignation. But the Christian must beware of letting his temper lead him into sin, as it easily can. "Do not let the sun go down on your anger"—never go to bed resentful. "And give no opportunity to the devil" (4:27). "Opportunity" is literally "room." It is the hot fit of anger that gives the Devil his chance; therefore we must give him no "room" in which he can work. "Let the thief no longer steal" (4:28). On the contrary, he should turn to honest work so that he may be able to help his needy neighbor. "Evil talk" (4:29), the next sin mentioned, is "bad language," the index of a dirty mind. What the Christian says should be "edifying," that is, helpful and constructive, and appropriate, "that it may impart grace to those who hear." In other words, a Christian's conversation should be at once pleasant to listen to and helpful to faith. For foul speech will "grieve the Holy Spirit of God, in whom you were sealed for the day of redemption" (4:30). A seal denotes proprietorship. God's Spirit within us is the sign that we belong to him, and that one day he means to redeem us fully.

Finally (4:31-32), Paul gathers all the unlovely and un-christian qualities into one sentence—"bitterness and wrath and anger and clamor and slander . . . with all malice"—and in the next one, lists the qualities which should replace them—kind-ness, compassion, and the forgiving spirit. As always, Paul grounds Christian conduct in Christian doctrine: "forgiving one another, as God in Christ forgave you." "God in Christ" means "God acting in Christ" (see II Cor. 5:19), with a reference to the Cross where God's forgiveness was supremely offered to men.

There is no real break at the end of chapter 4. Be forgiving, Paul had said, "as God in Christ forgave you." Now he goes on, saying in effect: "Copy God, for you are his children whom he loves. And you too must live in love, such love as Christ's—to the point of sacrifice."

Jesus had bidden his disciples copy God (Matt. 5:45)—to act "in their small corners" as God does in his big world. So Paul also counsels "an imitation of God," implying that we are most like God when we live in love. The love demanded is sacrificial love like Christ's (see John 13:34, the new commandment). "Christ loved us and gave himself up for us, a fragrant offering and sacrifice to God" (5:2). The metaphor here originated in the primitive notion that Deity rejoiced in the fragrance of the offered sacrifice. Paul is not here expounding a "sacrificial" the-ory of the Atonement but simply saying that Christ's giving of his life for us pleased God.

Then he warns his readers against sensuality (5:3). God's people must not even so much as mention "immorality . . . im-purity or covetousness." "Filthiness," which is obscenity, and "silly talk" are likewise forbidden (5:4). But why ban so ap-parently unobjectionable a thing as "levity"? Is there not a place in the Christian's life for "a little judicious levity"? Surely there is. What Paul is condemning here is a much more questionable "levity"—in fact, bawdiness. Instead, he calls for "thanksgiv-ing." Gratitude for God's grace is what he means. Thus the note of thanksgiving should keep sounding through the Christian's life.

Next (5:5), Paul tells them why they dare not be immoral.

Immorality will exclude a man from "the kingdom of Christ and of God"—from full and final salvation. With the immoral person he brackets "one who is covetous (that is, an idolator)." Covetousness in its widest sense is worship of Mammon; in its narrower sexual sense it is worship of the flesh.

The Christian, Paul continues in verses 6 and 7, will pay no heed to any specious deceiver who tells him otherwise. "These things," immoral actions, bring down God's wrath on "the sons of disobedience," the men who despise God and his laws. Christians should shun their company. "For once you were darkness, but now you are light in the Lord; walk as children of light" (5:8). "Light" is one of the great universal religious symbols which Christianity has appropriated, so that we talk of "seeing the light" (conversion). Christians "are light" because they live in the dawning of God's new era, the Kingdom of God, and serve a Lord who is "the Light of the world." Because they "are light" in that Lord, they must behave as "children of light." As always the indicative mood of the gospel carries with it its imperative. The parenthesis of verse 9 explains that such light is to be known by its moral fruit. In other words, truly converted people must manifest kindness, justice, and truth in their lives. So far from sharing in "the unfruitful works of darkness" (what a barren thing is evil!) they are bound to "expose" them (5:11). It is hard to tell precisely what Paul means by "the things that they do in secret" (5:12) and which are almost unmentionable. Perhaps he is thinking of some religious groups which secretly practiced unholy rites. What he does say is that exposure to the light is the best remedy against such deeds of darkness (see John 3:20).

The meaning of the first part of verse 13 is tolerably clear, that under the action of light there can be no secrecy. We may imagine a searchlight picking out in its beams some sinister object and revealing it in its stark ugliness. But in the last part of the verse the expression, "for anything that becomes visible is light," has puzzled interpreters. The point seems to be the transforming power of light. Let light play steadily on some dark object, and it will change it into its own likeness. So the effect of Christian goodness on a pagan society will be first to shame and then to purify it. At this point (5:14) the thought of the change from darkness to light reminds Paul of the hymn Christians often sang when a convert was baptized, and he quotes two lines:

"Awake, O sleeper, and arise from the dead,
    and Christ shall give you light."

It is a call to "wake up" from the pagan sleep of sin and death,
with the promise that Christ will then shine on the convert with
the saving light of his truth.

Next (5:15) comes a summons to Christian circumspectness
and "wise" dealing. Had not Christ himself told his disciples to
"be wise as serpents"? (Matt. 10:16). One of the ways in which
this wisdom can be shown is in "making the most of the time"
(literally, "buying up the critical time"). This is a metaphor
derived from commerce, bidding us make our selection to the
full from the opportunities of this life. We are to redeem time,
not try to escape from it, and are to miss no chance of turning
it to spiritual account. The phrase, "because the days are evil,"
gives the reason for this. The fact that contemporary moral
standards are low may become an excuse for many people to
lower their own standards. For the Christian the evilness of the
days will become a challenge to keep his standards up. Therefore,
instead of being "foolish," Paul says (5:17), Christians will seek
to find "what the will of the Lord is," and, having found it, will
do it. When we pray the Lord's Prayer and come to the third
petition, we should say: "Thy will be done—and done by me!"

Next (5:18), quoting Proverbs 23:31 in the Greek translation,
Paul bids his readers replace the so-called "fun of getting drunk"
by spiritual exhilaration. "Do not get drunk with wine, for that is
debauchery; but be filled with the Spirit." The Greek word translated "debauchery" is also used to describe the Prodigal Son's
downfall (Luke 15:13): drunkenness is the primrose path that
leads to degradation like his. The remedy is to "be filled with the
Spirit"—to let the Holy Spirit take full possession. Then, as now,
men drank too heavily. Indeed, in the cult of Dionysus the devotees used to seek communion with their god through intoxica-
tion. Doubtless the drinkers made the same excuses as their suc-
cessors make: the desire to escape from their troubles or to find
sociality. Is mere "prohibitionism" the cure? The true remedy,
Paul suggests, is the wholesome inspiration of Christian fellowship.

Such fellowship naturally finds expression in "spiritual songs"
(5:19). The Early Church, we need to remember, started on its
way singing. A wonderful new world of truth had swum into
their ken. New springs of emotion had been unsealed. What

wonder if they felt the need to create new hymns and spiritual songs? Here in this verse we see the beginnings of that Christian hymnody which has done as much as preaching to spread the gospel around the world. "Singing and making melody to the Lord with all your heart" suggests something of the fervor and glow of these earliest Christian services; it indicates as well that the Apostle liked "hearty" singing! Finally, such Christian singing should have one dominant motif, namely, thanksgiving: "always and for everything giving thanks in the name of our Lord Jesus Christ to God the Father" (5:20). Christian thankfulness should not be confined to Sunday worship; it should be evoked every day by everything the good God gives us; and it should ascend to heaven in the name and for the sake of the Lord who is our only mediator.

Third Charge: to Build Christian Homes (5:21—6:9)

The theme of the letter has been unity. Now Paul turns to the family groups which make up the Church, insisting that unity, like charity, begins at home.

"Be subject to one another out of reverence for Christ," he says (5:21). This command goes with what follows and sets mutual subordination as the rule in the Church. Paul's concept of subordination is not popular in these days when we never tire of affirming that all men are created equal and when there is much talk of the equality of the sexes. Yet, even in a worldly society, some must rule and others serve, and in the Church this principle of mutual subordination finds its exemplar in the One who "though he was in the form of God . . . emptied himself, taking the form of a servant" (Phil. 2:6-7).

The first example of this is in the words, "Wives, be subject to your husbands, as to the Lord" (5:22). This is hardly likely to please the Christian wives of today who hold firmly to the equality of the sexes! But only male arrogance will wish to interpret it with a moralistic literalism. The next verse gives the reason for this wifely submission: "For the husband is the head of the wife as Christ is the head of the church" (5:23). Headship means authority. The man's headship in the home corresponds to Christ's Headship in the Church and carries similar authority. But the analogy is not perfect, as Paul's addition makes plain: "and is himself its Savior."

Next, Paul bids the husbands love their wives, "as Christ

loved the church and gave himself up for her" (5:25)—that is, to the point of sacrifice. When the husband's duty is understood thus, Paul's previous command to the wife loses all offensiveness in modern ears. Who would find it hard to submit to sacrificial love? Having spoken of Christ's sacrificial love for the Church, Paul allows himself to add a sentence on Christ's purpose (5:26-27). It was to "sanctify" or consecrate the Church—to set her apart as holy for God's service (see John 17:19). He "cleansed" her, Paul says, "by the washing of water." In the East, before a bride goes to meet her bridegroom, she takes a ceremonial bath. So Christ cleansed his Church by the "washing" of baptism. "With the word" must refer to some confession of the Church's faith uttered at baptism. After the ceremonial bath the Eastern bride, clad in her loveliest garments, presents herself before her bridegroom. This explains the words, "that the church might be presented before him in splendor, without spot or wrinkle," without a trace of defilement or a mark of age. All this is surely a picture of the Church as God means her to be in his completed purpose.

With verse 28 Paul returns to his subject, which is the husband's love for his wife. "Even so husbands should love their wives as their own bodies." They are to love them, notice, not as they love their own bodies, but as being their own bodies. Husband and wife belong together as complementary parts of one personality, so that it can be said that "he who loves his wife loves himself." Verse 29 explains this: "The man who has learned to think of his wife as his own flesh will nourish and cherish her as Christ does the church." To clinch his point Paul quotes Genesis 2:24, laying all the stress on the last clause, "the two shall become one" (5:31). And this leads him to the theological speculation of verse 32, which has puzzled so many.

"This is a great mystery, and I take it to mean Christ and the church" (5:32). Human marriage, Paul says, is a symbol of a transcendental marriage. We might put his meaning thus: "This union between man and woman in one flesh is a profound symbol, because it points away beyond itself to an eternal reality— it is, in my view, a symbol of the spiritual union between Christ and his Church."

The nuptial metaphor, as it has been called, occurs frequently in the Bible to describe the relation between God or Christ and his people. We find it in the Old Testament, in Christ's words, and in Paul's theology. Perhaps we ought to make more of it today than we do. We all attend weddings. Why should we not try to maintain and preserve this contact between ordinary human life and God's mysteries?

"However," says Paul (5:33), returning from his speculation, the practical point is this: "let each one of you love his wife as himself, and let the wife see that she respects her husband." Only somebody with an exaggerated view of the equality of the sexes could take exception to this!

Paul now addresses the fathers and children. "Children, obey your parents in the Lord" (6:1). The child's primary duty to his parents is obedience, a timely reminder in these days when we tend to regard the freedom of the child as an absolute. But the phrase "in the Lord" shows that it is to be obedience in a Christ-centered family circle. Such obedience is morally "right," and is enjoined in the fifth comandment (Exod. 20:12; Deut. 5:16), described as "the first commandment with a promise" (6:2). This may mean: the fifth is the first of the Ten Commandments carrying an explicit promise, namely, of well-being and longevity. But if "first" means "primary," we might interpret thus: "This, for children, is a primary commandment, accompanied with a promise."

Paul turns next to the fathers (6:4). "Do not provoke your children to anger" means, "Do not exasperate them by teasing, or ridicule, or persistent scolding." On the contrary, "bring them up in the discipline and instruction of the Lord." The contrast is between the nagging of foolish parents and the "sweet reasonableness" of truly Christian ones. The Greek word rendered "discipline" means "education." This is the earliest reference to what we would call Christian education in the home. A verse like this should make every careless Christian parent ask himself: "Will my children, later in life, wandering about in unbelief, rise up to curse me because, intent on giving them the stone of worldly success, I forgot to give them the Bread of Life?"

Paul next considers the relations between slaves and masters (6:5). Slavery was the great blot on ancient civilization, and enemies of Christianity often complain that the New Testament does not denounce it root and branch. It is fair, however, to reply that such a frontal attack on it by a minority of people without political rights would have been a mere tilting at windmills; and that the impulse for its ultimate abolition came, not from our critics, but from Christians. Slaves are to obey their earthly masters, says Paul, "with fear and trembling" (with solicitous concern), and "in singleness of heart" (with complete loyalty), remembering that, when they do so, they are serving Christ. Paul is less concerned with "the rights of man" than with everyone's duty to serve the Lord; yet his words imply that the slave is no mere chattel, as he was regarded in Roman society, but a full moral personality, responsible ultimately to Christ alone. The slaves' service should not be "eye-service"—working only when they think their master's eye is on them; or men-pleasing—working only to court human favor. They should work willingly as in the eye of the Great Employer who will, at the Judgment Day, consider only the intrinsic worth of a man's performance (6:6-8).

"Masters, do the same to them" (6:9). In civil law slaves had no rights at all. In the Christian fellowship, however, the obligations are two-way. Masters are to show their slaves the same clemency and consideration as they expect to receive. For over all hangs "the democracy of Judgment Day," and the Master who is Lord of both earthly master and slave, will have no favorites then.

Fourth Charge: to Put on the Armor of God (6:10-20)

Paul has been thinking of the Church as it is, and as it is to be, from within. Now he describes the warfare it must wage from without.

"Finally, be strong in the Lord and in the strength of his might" (6:10). The secret of this Christ-inspired strength Paul himself knew well, as Philippians 4:13 shows. The Christian is called to fight against "the wiles of the devil," which are temptations to sin in every shape and form. For this he needs "the whole armor of God" (6:11): the complete suit of mail and weapons which God supplies. Before he describes them, Paul defines the enemy to be fought. "We are not contending against flesh and blood" (6:12). Our adversaries are more than human; demonic powers are arrayed against us. "Principalities" and "powers" represent the beings of the unseen world already referred to by Paul. With them he now sets "the world rulers of this present darkness"— the mighty angelic beings who hold sway over this material world of darkness, exerting a malign influence on human affairs. These adversaries are all summed up as "the spiritual hosts of wickedness in the heavenly places"—in the invisible world. What are we to make of them? Is it enough to say that Paul, as a first-century man, believes in the reality of the Devil and the demonic, and that enlightened twentieth-century men have no need of any such hypothesis? Certainly we are not necessarily committed to all the details of Paul's "diabolology." Yet we cannot dismiss all of it as outmoded superstition. Depth psychology in our day has revealed demonic depths in the soul of man, and two World Wars have laid bare the vast and radical range of evil. As a result, Paul's diagnosis of our predicament commands a new respect from many of our secular thinkers, and not a few Christian theologians take the Devil with new seriousness.

For this "real fight," Paul says, there is only one sure safe-guard, which is to equip ourselves with the armor of God (6:13). Then, "in the evil day"—any time when wickedness comes to a head—we "may be able to withstand"—to resist resolutely—and "having done all"—having made all proper preparations—to "stand" fast.

The next four verses (6:14-17) describe the armor God gives the Christian soldier. Six pieces are mentioned: the belt, the breastplate, the shoes, the shield, the helmet, and the sword. We need not press their precise significance too closely. The helmet and the breastplate come from Isaiah 59:17; the shoes recall Isaiah 52:7.

First, the Christian is to belt himself with "truth" or faithful-ness. His breastplate is "righteousness," uprightness of life. His feet are to wear "the equipment of the gospel of peace." Equip-ment means literally "readiness"—the Christian's readiness to carry the good news of peace everywhere, like a Roman soldier at his general's bidding. In order to ward off "the flaming darts of the evil one"—that is, the attacks of the Devil—he carries "the shield of faith." Paul's readers would think of the oblong Roman shield, made of wood and covered with hide, which absorbed the adversary's darts and protected its wearer's body. On his head is "the helmet of salvation," and in his right hand "the sword of the Spirit" defined as "the word of God." "The sword which the Holy Spirit supplies" is Paul's meaning; but we must not take "the word of God" to mean simply Holy Scripture. The "word" is the utterance God gives his servants. Jesus, foreseeing future troubles, had told his disciples, "The Holy Spirit will teach you . . . what you ought to say" (Luke 12:12). This is what Paul means here. In the day of battle the Christian soldier may rely on God for utterance to fit the occasion. So Peter answered Gamaliel, and Luther his inquisitors. Finally (6:18) the ceaseless vigilance which the soldier must observe is associated with prayer, as also in the Garden of Gethsemane (Mark 14:38).

The last two verses of this section (6:19-20) recall us to Paul's situation. He bids his readers pray for him and for his mission, that he may not himself lack courage, even in jail, to proclaim boldly "the mystery of the gospel," the open secret of God's plan to reconcile creation in Christ. The phrase "ambassador in chains" reminds them that, though a prisoner, he represents Christ the King in the Imperial City.

CONCLUSION
Ephesians 6:21-24

Paul commends Tychicus, the bearer of the letter, to all Christians in Asia Minor to whom this circular letter goes. He will give them all the news of himself they want (see Col. 4:7-9).

The benediction, as befits a circular letter, is in the third person and addressed to the whole Christian fellowship. "Peace" recalls one of the great themes of the letter. "Love with faith" reminds us of Galatians 5:6. The last word of the final verse is difficult. Literally the Greek means "in imperishableness," which sounds like a sonorous way of saying "for ever." "Grace be with all lovers of our Lord Jesus Christ for ever." And how better could this sublime epistle end?

THE LETTER OF PAUL TO THE

PHILIPPIANS

INTRODUCTION

If there were a competition to decide which is the most beauti-
ful of Paul's letters, the odds would be strongly on Philippians.
It could also lay fair claim to being the most "Pauline" in the
sense of revealing to us the man Paul in all his many-sided character—his courage, humility, independence, and serenity. So
true is this that no reputable modern interpreter of Philippians
doubts that Paul wrote the letter. We are thus delivered at the
outset from all questions of authorship. The real questions at
issue in Philippians are where and when Paul wrote the letter.
But before these points are discussed, a word should be said about
Philippi and Paul's contacts with it.

Paul and Philippi

The city of Philippi, now no longer existent, lay in East Macedonia—the northern part of Greece—and derived its name from
Philip, father of Alexander the Great, who had founded it in
368 B.C. on a site formerly known as *Krenides* or "Springs." He
chose his site well, as a glance at a map will show. A range of
hills divides Europe from Asia, and just at Philippi the range dips
down into a pass. Philippi, therefore, commanded the great road
—the *Via Egnatia,* as it was called—from Europe to Asia. No
doubt it was for this geographical reason that in 42 B.C. Philippi
saw one of the decisive battles of history, when Antony and
Octavian (later to become the Emperor Augustus) defeated and
slew Brutus and Cassius, the murderers of Caesar. The other fact
of interest is that the victors, aware of the city's strategic position,
turned it into a Roman colony by settling many of their veterans
there. In a Roman colony the inhabitants did most things in a
Roman way. Not only did they wear Roman dress, but their
whole economy and law were based on a Roman pattern. Thus
Philippi became a miniature of Rome, a fact no doubt in Paul's
mind when he wrote in Philippians 3:20, "Our commonwealth is

in heaven." The word translated "commonwealth" is, perhaps more accurately, "our capital city."

It was about the year A.D. 50 that Paul, in company with Silas, Timothy, and probably Luke (the appearance of the first of the so-called "we-passages" at Acts 16:10 would seem to indicate that Luke was present), crossed the Aegean Sea and landed in Macedonia not far from Philippi. The story of their mission in Philippi is told in Acts 16. We learn there how Lydia of Thyatira, the dealer in purple, was won to the faith, and how Paul's cure of a slave-girl with psychic powers so incensed her owners that they denounced Paul and his friends to the magistrates who, after scourging them, threw them in prison and put them in the stocks. After the prisoners had been providentially released by an earthquake, their jailer was converted and baptized along with his family. Then the magistrates, on learning that they were Roman citizens, were glad to apologize for the unlawful scourging and to beg them to leave the town.

So Paul sowed the seed of the gospel in Philippi, and a splendid harvest it was to yield. For the little company of Christians who had their first meeting in Lydia's house grew into a church which was dearer to Paul than any other.

Thus the years went by. Once and again Paul revisited Philippi (Acts 20:1-6; II Cor. 2:12-18; 7:5-7); and the church there, though it did not escape persecution (Phil. 1:27-30), prospered. At length Paul's journeying came to an abrupt end: he was arrested in Jerusalem and, after two years' detention in Caesarea, was sent to Rome to stand his trial before the Emperor. There for two years he remained in a kind of free custody awaiting the Emperor's pleasure.

But even in that ancient world, without telegraph or a decent postal system, news traveled fast, and one day the Christians in Philippi heard with dismay of Paul's fate. Without more ado they "passed the hat" (as we would say), and some weeks later there arrived in Rome a man from Philippi, Epaphroditus, with a present of money for the Apostle and the offer of his own personal services. Unfortunately, while serving Paul, Epaphroditus fell seriously ill (Phil. 2:25-27). When he was better, Paul resolved to send him back to Philippi with a letter of thanks for the gift. The letter which he wrote is our epistle. Since his trial seemed imminent (Phil. 2:17), we surmise that it was written near the end of the two years of Roman imprisonment, about A.D. 62.

Rome or Ephesus?

The situation sketched above is the commonly accepted view of when and where Philippians was written. But in the last fifty years a number of students have contended that not only Philippians but all the "Prison Epistles" were written in *Ephesus,* not in Rome. If so, these letters must have been written six or seven years earlier, during Paul's three years' stay in Ephesus.

But, it may be objected, Acts has no record of Paul's being imprisoned in Ephesus. This is one weakness in the theory. We *know* that Paul was imprisoned in Rome; we have only circumstantial evidence that he was imprisoned in Ephesus. What does it amount to? We need not pay much attention to the fact that guides in Ephesus today will point out a tower as Paul's prison, or that the apocryphal *Acts of Paul and Thekla* preserves a similar tradition. Two passages in Paul's own letters are more impressive. In one (I Cor. 15:32) he tells us that he "fought with beasts at Ephesus"; in another (II Cor. 1:8-10), that while "in Asia" (presumably Ephesus) he had been very near death. Had either of these passages contained the words "bonds" or "prison," the case for an Ephesian imprisonment would have been very strong indeed.

At this point supporters of the traditional view may remind us of what looks like clear evidence for Rome. Does not Paul allude to the "praetorian guard" (Phil. 1:13) and to "the saints . . . of Caesar's household"? (Phil. 4:22). Surely phrases like these settle the question? But it is not so; for inscriptions have shown that "praetorians" as well as members of the Imperial Civil Service (which is what "Caesar's household" means) were to be found in Ephesus. Nor is this all; certain evidences in the letter itself seem to point away from Rome to Ephesus. One point against Rome is the fact that, while Paul after his journey to Jerusalem was planning to go *west*—to Rome and perhaps Spain (Rom. 15:23-29)—in Philippians he is planning a return to Philippi (Phil. 2:24). A positive point in favor of Ephesus is the fact that Philippians 2:19-30 implies frequent comings and goings between Paul's prison and Philippi (four journeys are implied). Now Rome, in point of traveling time, was at least three times farther away from Philippi than was Ephesus. Arguments which seek to show that the theology of Philippians is more like that of the letters Paul wrote while in Ephesus (I and II Corinthians) than like that of Colossians and Ephesians, are much more speculative. Nevertheless, when we have weighed all the pros and cons for Rome and Ephesus, we must candidly admit that the Ephesian theory is no wild fantasy. The question therefore must be left open. If Philippians was written from Ephesus, its date will be about A.D. 55; if it came from Rome, the year A.D. 62 seems likely. It remains to add that the worth of the letter for us today is not in the least affected by the answer we give to this question.

Purpose and Integrity

The occasion of the letter is not doubtful. Paul's primary purpose when he wrote Philippians was to say "Thank you" to his old friends for their generosity to himself (Phil. 4:10-20). But he also used the occasion to persuade them to mend certain little rifts appearing in their fellowship (2:1-4; 4:2-3), and to give them the news about Epaphroditus and about himself (1:12-26; 2:25-30).

Now something should be said concerning the unity of the letter. Up to chapter 3:1 all has been good feeling. But at this point two things give us pause. First, Paul writes a "finally" as though he were drawing to a close; and then, without any warning, explodes into a fierce denunciation of the Judaizers: "Look out for the dogs . . ." For these reasons some scholars have held that our epistle really contains bits of two letters. They say that 3:2—4:3 is a letter of warning and thanks which he sent to Philippi soon after the arrival of Epaphroditus; whereas 1:1—3:1 is the letter Paul gave to Epaphroditus to take home with him. One weakness of this "partitionist" theory is that its supporters cannot agree on the verse where the first letter ended. Another is the fact that the Greek word rendered "finally" did not necessarily have the finality we are apt to give to the English word. Often it served simply as a phrase of transition to a new topic. And, lastly, sudden changes of tone in a letter of Paul's are not unparalleled. All that we need to explain this one is the receipt of bad news from Philippi. The case for partition is far from proved. We may well maintain the integrity of the letter.

The Value of the Letter

What is the value of this letter for us today? Like every other letter written by Paul, we value it because we have in it an authentic record of the spiritual experience of one whom many acknowledge as the supreme expert on the Christian faith. For the letter sheds light, not only on the little church in Philippi which came nearest to being Paul's "ideal congregation," but also on the Apostle himself and his gospel.

It has been said that Philippians gives us the truest, loveliest, and most complete picture we have of Paul the Christian. This is true, and part of the explanation is the *intimacy* of the letter. A friend is writing to friends (so that, in the Address, he even dispenses with his usual title of "apostle"), and the whole letter is cast in almost conversational tones. Only once or twice, as in his warnings against the Judaizers (3:2-3) and the Christian libertines (3:18-19), does he, so to speak, "raise his voice" and let indignation come into it. For the rest, this letter exhibits the *gentler* side of Paul's nature, tenderness predominating over sternness and suffusing the whole with the mellowness of one who has fought his battles and now, nearing the end of his course, finds his life filled with peace and confidence.

What, then, are the aspects of Paul's many-sided character which shine out clearest in Philippians? In first place must surely go his unquenchable Christian serenity and *joy*—"I rejoice, and you must rejoice too"—which, though he writes from prison, is the theme of many of his exhortations. Better than any other of his letters Philippians exemplifies the truth of the dictum that "God's best servants have never been sad people"; that through all trials and tribulations Christian cheerfulness has a way of breaking in. Hardly less striking is the noble *humility* of the man Paul in this letter. The great passage in Philippians 2:5-11 holds up as example for the Philippians the divine humility of Christ. But the Savior's humility has its human counterpart in Paul's moving personal testimony in chapter 3, when he tells us how he gladly renounced all his precious Jewish privileges and all his proud religious attainments as a Pharisee and counted them as refuse in comparison with the surpassing worth of knowing Christ Jesus as Lord (3:4-11). The Apostle could, at times, boast (see II Cor. 10:1—12:13); but now, in Philippians, humility has overcome pride: "Not that I have already obtained this or am already perfect; but I press on to make it my own, because Christ Jesus has made me his own" (3:12). To serenity and humility we must add *tact;* and if an illustration of this is needed, it is the fine delicacy with which he says "Thank you" to the Philippians for their gift of money to himself (4:10-20). All these Christian graces flow from one source—the grace of Christ. Here is the secret of Paul's power and greatness as a Christian. Christ is "the master-light of all his seeing"; Christ is his Savior in all the chances and changes of this mortal life; Christ is the divine Companion in whose strength he lives, and into whose presence he will go when death comes. "For to me to live is Christ" (1:21). "I count everything as loss because of the surpassing worth of knowing Christ Jesus my Lord" (3:8). "I can do all things in him who strengthens me" (4:13). "My desire is to depart and be with Christ, for that is far better" (1:23).

The great passages of this letter come in 1:19-26 where he surveys his prospects of living or dying; in 2:6-11 where he preserves for us a noble hymn to Christ in his humiliation and exaltation; in 3:4-16 where he tells us how he gladly gave up all his proud Jewish privileges for the knowledge of Christ; and in 4:4-13 where a summons to rejoice is followed by another to think noble thoughts, and where he lets us into the secret of his "independence," which is dependence upon Another.

But the real theme of this letter is: "I rejoice, and you must rejoice too." Philippians is a paean from prison.

OUTLINE

Philippians is a real letter and therefore not readily subjected to precise analysis, as though it were a theological treatise with an argument that marches to a conclusion. But the following scheme will show its contents:

Introduction. Philippians 1:1-11
  The Address (1:1-2)
  Thanksgiving and Prayer (1:3-11)

Paul in Prison. Philippians 1:12-26
  The Progress of the Gospel (1:12-18)
  The Apostle's Dilemma (1:19-26)

The Christian Life. Philippians 1:27—2:18
  Call to Worthy Living (1:27-30)
  Call to Unity and Humility (2:1-5)
  The Christ Hymn (2:6-11)
  Work Out Your Own Salvation (2:12-18)

Paul's Plans. Philippians 2:19-30

Paul's Apologia. Philippians 3:1-21
  Warning Against Judaizers (3:1-3)
  Retrospect and Prospect (3:4-16)
  Beware of Libertines (3:17-21)

Final Admonitions. Philippians 4:1-9

The Present from Philippi. Philippians 4:10-20

Greetings and Benediction. Philippians 4:21-23

COMMENTARY

INTRODUCTION
Philippians 1:1-11

The Address (1:1-2)

Brief as it is, the address reveals the controlling passion of Paul's life, his complete devotion to the Savior, who is mentioned no less than three times in two verses.

Along with his own name as sender he couples that of his trusty coadjutor Timothy. They are both "servants of Christ Jesus," the word "servants" suggesting not only the idea of a special calling (as it had done when applied to the Old Testament prophets), but also a complete devotion to their common Lord.

The addressees are "all the saints in Christ Jesus who are at Philippi, with the bishops and deacons." For Philippi and the church there, see the Introduction. The first point to notice here is that "saints" in its New Testament sense means not people wearing halos but committed Christians. Like the word for "church" the term "saints" describes Christians as belonging to the new and true people of God who are heirs to the promises made to Old Israel. Of course they are summoned to become holy as God their Father is holy; but the stress is on their consecration rather than on any moral perfection. With the word "saints" Paul joins his famous phrase "in Christ Jesus," in order to define their "sainthood." The phrase describes those who are not only in communion with the living Christ but are members of the new community of which he is the Head.

The real crux here is the phrase "with the bishops and deacons." The words seem to describe two kinds of church officials, and many scholars wonder whether such officials existed in Paul's lifetime. Other references to "bishops" in the New Testament will be found in Acts 20:28; I Timothy 3:2; and Titus 1:7. The only other use of the word "deacon" in a *technical* sense is to be found in I Timothy 3:8-13. What shall we say of the phrase as a whole? There is no reason why the word translated here as "bishops," meaning "overseers," should not have been applied to certain elders (or presbyters) in the church at Philippi, to whom had been assigned administrative duties. (It is agreed that in the New Testament "elder" and "bishop" refer to the same office, the former stressing status, the latter function.) If this is so, the deacons must have been their assistants, perhaps specially charged with financial matters. Paul mentions them here because (we may surmise) they had been the persons who actually transmitted the Philippian church's gift to Paul (Phil. 4:10-13).

Now note the greeting. By changing a few letters Paul substitutes for the customary greeting (*chairein*, a kind of opening "cheerio") a word of similar sound (*charis*), the great word "grace," meaning the wonderful kindness of God to sinners. With it he joins the normal Jewish greeting of "peace." The grace and peace come "from God our Father and the Lord Jesus Christ"; that is, from the Supreme Being whom Jesus had revealed as *Abba*, Father, and from the Messiah Jesus who by his resurrection had become Lord (2:9-11).

Thanksgiving and Prayer (1:3-11)

The thanksgiving is usual, but the warmth of it is unusual because the church at Philippi had a special place in Paul's heart. It came nearer than any other to being his ideal congregation.

Paul cannot pray for his Christian converts in Philippi without giving God thanks for them and rejoicing. (Compare what he has to say about the Galatians!) Joy is, indeed, the dominant note of this letter, which contains no less than nineteen words for it. The immediate cause of Paul's joy is their "partnership in the gospel from the first day until now" (1:5). The basic meaning of "partnership" is "sharing." What kind of sharing has Paul in mind here? The idea of their united Christian action cannot be excluded, but he is properly thinking mostly of the very tangible expression of their Christian fellowship which had evoked this letter—their gift of money. "From the first day" refers to the time when they became Christians, that is, about A.D. 50 (see Acts 16).

For this reason Paul is sure that "he [God] who began a good work in you"—their growth in grace—will perfect it "at the day of Jesus Christ" (1:6). This is the day of God's final victory in Christ, the day when, as the Creed says, "He shall come to judge the quick and the dead."

It is altogether right that Paul should feel this way about the Philippians since he regards them as co-sharers with himself in grace, "both in my imprisonment and in the defense and confirmation of the gospel" (1:7). The Greek word here translated "defense" often carried a judicial meaning, standing for a defense against a regular charge. If this is the meaning, we might paraphrase Paul's words, "whether in prison or standing before my judges." But the word may equally well describe Paul's vigorous championing of the gospel against its enemies.

The next verse throbs with tender affection for his converts: "I yearn for you all with the affection of Christ Jesus." It is as if not Paul but Christ himself were living in the Apostle. Every true pastor has felt something of this affection for his people.

The affection passes into a prayer that their love and understanding of the truth will go on increasing. Paul wants heart and head to grow together. To their "love" they must add "knowledge" (of God) "and all discernment"—all spiritual perception. Here is a test that every Christian congregation might profitably put to themselves: Are we growing year by year (a) in Christian love and (b) in understanding of the gospel? And if not, what do all our increases in money and members signify?

The end of it all is that they may "approve what is excellent, and may be pure and blameless for the day of Christ" (1:10). Here the Greek permits two translations: either "approve what is excellent" as in the Revised Standard Version, or "test things that differ"—that is, distinguish between good and evil, or perhaps between what is good and what is better (see Rom. 2:18). In either case it is a prayer that they may know what is essential in religion. It is a call to put first things first. We all know Christians who get "worked up" about nonessentials to the neglect of fundamentals.

What does Paul mean in the next verse (1:11) by "the fruits of righteousness which come through Jesus Christ"? He means what he calls elsewhere "the fruit of the Spirit": love, joy, peace, and the like (Gal. 5:22). Paul had no time for a righteousness—an acceptance with God—which did not issue in good works and lovely virtues. Faith, he said, should work through love (Gal. 5:6). Tabitha of Joppa, as described in Acts 9:36, was one such example: "She was full of good works and acts of charity." Her faith had flowered in love.

PAUL IN PRISON

Philippians 1:12-26

The Progress of the Gospel (1:12-18)

God can use, Paul says, even apparently untoward happenings like the imprisonment of his servant to further the gospel (1:12; see also Gen. 45:8 for the case of Joseph and his brethren). Paul explains that the whole "praetorian guard" now realizes that his "imprisonment is for Christ." The last five words mean literally: "my bonds have become manifest-in-Christ." The meaning is that "the whole praetorium" can see for themselves that his imprisonment is for Christ's sake and not for any crime. But what is meant by "the whole praetorium"? The Revised Standard Version takes it to refer to the famous Imperial bodyguards, some 10,000 strong, whose headquarters were in Rome. This may well be right. If so, Paul's imprisonment gave him the chance of evangelizing the crack regiment of the Roman army. But the word may also describe a general's or governor's residence. Nowadays we should probably say, "Government House." There were such Government Houses in the Roman provinces; for example, in Ephesus. The phrase, therefore, does not tie our letter to Rome. It might also mean "the whole of Government House" in Ephesus, for we know from inscriptions that there were Imperial civil servants and also "praetorians" in that city. This point will be discussed again when we come to consider who "the saints . . . of Caesar's household" were (4:22).

Paul proceeds (1:14) to describe the influence of his imprisonment on "the brethren," meaning the Christians round about him. The majority, he says, taking courage from his own demeanor in prison, have been emboldened to speak "the word of God without fear." (Note: to "speak the word of God" is obviously the same thing as to "preach Christ" in the next verse. Could anything show more clearly that for Paul, as for John, Christ is the Word of God?) Observe the implication that all Christians have the privilege of proclaiming the gospel, not merely certain select people. This is what we might call "the prophethood of all believers" (see Num. 11:29, "Would that all the LORD's people were prophets . . . !"). Is not this a part of "the apostolate of the laity" on which we are placing increasing emphasis today?

But there are preachers and preachers (1:15): some who preach for the right reasons, and others who preach for wrong ones. The former act out of "good will" (to Paul and his cause), and are motivated by "love," because they know that Paul is in prison for the gospel's sake, and its defense. But who are the preachers who act out of "envy and rivalry"? Obviously they are men who bore some ill will to Paul, since they act "out of partisanship, not sincerely"—that is, for their own selfish ends and with mixed motives. These must have been Judaizers whose successful making of converts might be calculated to "afflict" or annoy Paul in his prison. Remembering the Letter to the Galatians, we might have expected Paul to denounce them out of hand. But, resisting this temptation, he displays a fine magnanimity. "What then? Only that in every way, whether in pretense or in truth, Christ is proclaimed" (1:18). It is as if Paul said, "I do not care much for their interpretation of the gospel. But better an imperfect gospel than none at all." The preaching of Christ is the main thing, and in that "the ambassador in bonds" rejoices and will rejoice. What unquenchable serenity!

The Apostle's Dilemma (1:19-26)

In this paragraph Paul surveys his prospects of survival, weighing the pros and cons. His first sentence asserts his conviction that he will be vindicated. Through their "prayers and the help of the Spirit," which is Christ's gift, "this [the present situation] will turn out for my deliverance" (1:19). Mark these last words; they are the words of Job 13:16 in the Septuagint version. Paul is solacing his spirit by comparing his lot with that of the patriarch. He is saying in effect: "Like Job, my own consciousness of integrity, of being right in all that has brought me where I am, warrants my confidence that like him I shall be vindicated."

This confidence matches his own "eager expectation" (a vivid word meaning "watching with outstretched head") that, so far from being ashamed, he will, in the present crisis, bravely honor his Savior in his own person (literally, "body"), whether in life or death (1:20). If God wills to spare him, he will magnify his Lord by further bodily suffering in his service; but if martyrdom be his lot, he will honor Christ by the way in which he yields up his life.

Then comes a great utterance: "For to me to live is Christ,

and to die is gain" (1:21). "Life means Christ to me," he confesses, "and if Christ were taken out of mine, there would be nothing left." Was there ever such a Christocentric man? Yet, even so, he continues, death will be *gain*. Why? Because death is the gateway to the immediate presence of Christ.

Yet, though such a state is "far better" (see verse 23), the issue for Paul is not clear. There is, after all, the alternative: "life in the flesh," that is, release and survival with all it offers of further fruitful service in evangelism. (In verse 22 the Revised Standard Version probably gives the correct sense of some rather obscure Greek. Paul will not have his readers suppose that he is pining for death.) Death or life—which shall it be? "I cannot tell," he answers. His case, as an old commentator put it, is like that of a loving wife summoned to the side of a husband living abroad and yet loath to leave her children, so that she is in a muse and doubt about what to do. "I am hard pressed between the two," he says (1:23). More literally the meaning is, "I am hemmed in from two sides." We would say, "I am torn in two directions." On the one hand, his own "desire" is "to depart [literally "break camp"] and be with Christ, for that is far better." Whatever Paul may earlier have believed about "sleeping" till Christ returned (see I Thess. 4:13-17 and I Cor. 15:51-52), he now holds that death will usher him straight into Christ's presence. (Compare Christ's promise, Luke 23:43, to the penitent criminal: "Today you will be with me in Paradise." See also II Corinthians 5:8.) What is the heart of the Christian hope? Is it not to be "with Christ"? Christ had prayed that his disciples might be where he was (John 17:24). Do we need to know more than that we shall thus be with him? On the other hand, says Paul (1:24), his continued existence on earth will better serve his converts. No mock modesty blinds this great servant of Christ to their need of him.

And with this, though the hard facts seem against it, there comes to Paul the strong presentiment that this is what will actually happen: "I know that I shall remain and continue with you all, for your progress and joy in the faith" (1:25). If this be so, when he returns to Philippi they will have ample cause for exulting in him "in Christ Jesus"—in that blessed fellowship which redeems all boasting from mere braggadocio.

THE CHRISTIAN LIFE
Philippians 1:27—2:18

Call to Worthy Living (1:27-30)

Here begins a "word of exhortation" which extends to 2:18. The principle of *noblesse oblige*—that men who have experienced God's mercy must live up to their high calling—runs through Paul's letters. An example is his exhortation in 1:27, "Let your manner of life be worthy of the gospel of Christ."

His one concern, whether he is with them or away from them, is that they should act unitedly, "with one mind striving side by side for the faith of the gospel" (1:27). The metaphor in the verb comes from the Greek games and describes an intensive activity. "Faith" here is on the way to becoming a technical term for Christianity, just as we talk sometimes of "the Faith." The call to unity is necessary because, as we shall see later, little rifts and tensions had begun to disfigure the Christian community in Philippi and because, as Paul goes on to say, a united front was the only right attitude in face of opponents who were threatening them. (Would that Christians today, amid their denominational differences, could see the wisdom of presenting a united front to the foes who face them!)

Who are the opponents mentioned in verse 28? They might be Jews ill disposed to the gospel. More probably they are heathen antagonists. In any case, the fearlessness of the Christians would be to them "a clear omen . . . of their destruction." Such enemies would see that the strength of the Christians could come only from superhuman sources. They would say to themselves, reversing Paul's question, "If God is against us, who can be for us?" And, noting the demeanor of the Philippian Christians, they would conclude that God must certainly be "for" such people.

For, Paul continues, "it has been granted to you that for the sake of Christ you should not only believe in him but also suffer for his sake" (1:29). Clearly Paul's readers had been undergoing persecution. Are some inclined to complain against their lot? Then, Paul says, let them realize that they are really favored persons! It is the Christian's privilege to suffer for his Savior. Let him welcome this privilege. Is this hard doctrine for soft Christians? Yes, but no doctrine has better warrant in the New Testament, which, from the time that Christ called his disciples to take up the cross right to the Book of Revelation, insists again and again, "No cross, no crown."

"Besides," Paul adds, "I am in it with you" (see 1:30). You are "engaged in the same conflict [struggle, another figure from the games] which you saw [see Acts 16:19-24] and now hear to be mine." Life, said Epictetus, is like an Olympic festival, and we are God's athletes to whom he has given the chance of showing of what stuff we are made. The Christian ought to be able to say that too, but with even more conviction. "Come, son," said the French veteran to the young recruit trembling on the brink of battle, "and you and I will do something fine for France." So Paul says, in effect, to the Philippians: "The battle is on for you and me. Let us do something fine for Christ."

Call to Unity and Humility (2:1-5)

Even Paul's "ideal" congregation contained "difficult" people. These verses clearly imply some disharmony in the church at Philippi. The remedy, Paul tells them, is to forget themselves, think on their neighbors, and be humble like Christ.

The moving plea of verses 1-2 may be thus expanded to make its meaning clear:

"If your experience in Christ makes any appeal to you, if love exerts any persuasion on you, if your fellowship in the Holy Spirit has any living reality, if you have any affection and sympathy in your heart, listen to me and obey. You have given me joy hitherto. Now fill my cup of gladness to the brim."

This they will do by "being of the same mind, having the same love, being in full accord and of one mind" (2:2). They should "do nothing from selfishness or conceit, but in humility count others better" than themselves (2:3). "Humility" translates a Greek word not used with approval before the New Testament. The Greek moralists took a poor view of humility. It was Christ who made it a mark of the noblest character.

The cure for their dissensions, Paul says, is selflessness. They are humbly to "count others better" than themselves, and, forgetting their own interests, consult those of others (2:4). In short, Paul is saying, "You should have the same disposition among yourselves as you have in your communion with Christ Jesus." Paul wishes them to practice in the life of the Christian community the spirit produced in their hearts by their fellowship with their Lord. And he proceeds to point them to the supreme example.

The Christ Hymn (2:6-11)

These six verses are held by most modern scholars to be one of the very earliest Christian hymns, sung perhaps by Christians in Antioch or Damascus, and quoted here by Paul as a modern preacher might weave some verses from a hymn, say, by Charles Wesley, into the fabric of his sermon.

Technicalities are forbidden in a commentary of this kind; but there should be some indication of the reasons for believing this to be an early hymn.

First, the section breaks the flow of Paul's exhortation and reads like an inserted passage.

Second, it has the liturgical style of a hymn, with its rhythms, balanced clauses, and parallelism, so that it falls easily into six stanzas, of three lines each.

Third, it contains at least five words not found elsewhere in Paul.

Fourth, its doctrine, especially its conception of Christ as the Servant of God, reminding us of the early speeches of Acts, suggests something really early and before the time of Paul. (Paul made little, if any, use of this doctrine.)

We may arrange and translate the hymn thus:

I	Who, being originally in the likeness of God, Did not count parity with God Something to be seized;	
II	But poured himself out, Taking a servant's likeness, Being made like men;	(Isa. 53:12) (Isa. 53)
III	And being found in fashion as a man, He humbled himself, Becoming obedient unto death, (Yes, and death on a cross!)	(Isa. 53:7) (Isa. 53:12)
IV	Therefore God highly exalted him, And conferred on him the name— The name that is above every name;	(Isa. 52:13)
V	That at the name of Jesus Every knee might bow, Of beings in heaven, on earth, and in the nether world,	

VI And every tongue confess:
"Jesus Christ is Lord,"
To the glory of God the Father.

Notice especially the five echoes of the last of the "Servant Songs" in Isaiah (Isa. 52:13—53:12). The fifth stanza also echoes Isaiah 45:23—

"To me every knee shall bow,
every tongue shall swear."

The reference to the "cross" at the end of the third stanza is probably Paul's own comment.

Now let us consider the interpretation. Before we can understand the hymn, we must note not only the five references to the Suffering Servant but also two references to the Book of Genesis. For "the likeness of God" recalls that Adam was made in God's likeness (Gen. 1:26-27), and "parity with God" recalls the words of the serpent to the woman, "You will be like God" (Gen. 3:5).

The theme of the hymn is Jesus, the Second Adam who, conquering the temptation to which the First Adam fell, chose the role of the Suffering Servant, and for his obedience unto death was highly exalted by God and made Lord of all created things.

The First Adam, who was created in God's likeness, sought to *seize* parity with God, and through his disobedience lost the glorious image of his Maker. But the Second Adam, Christ, who is the Heavenly Man, although he pre-existed in the true likeness of God, humbled himself obediently and accepted the status of a servant—the Servant of the Lord. Triumphing over the temptation to which the First Adam succumbed, he chose the way of meek submission to God's will, which ended in a cross. This obedience is the crucial factor in the drama of which the hymn tells. It reverses Adam's primal disobedience and leads to Christ's exaltation by the Father. The universal dominion promised to the First Adam was forfeited by his disobedience. It is restored to the Second Adam for his obedience.

Some of the detailed expressions in the hymn, as they appear in the Revised Standard Version, are of special interest.

"Though he was in the form of God" has a Greek verb which means "existing originally." It refers to Christ's preincarnate state. The "form" is the "likeness" of God (Gen. 1:26). It is a synonym for another Greek word meaning "image" or "likeness," and both represent the Hebrew word used in Genesis. When it is said that Christ pre-existed in the likeness of God, it does not mean that Christ was a mere copy or reflection; it means that he was "the visible representation" of the essence of the original—of God the Father. On the phrase "equality with God" see Genesis 3:5. "A thing to be grasped" means a prize or a "catch."

"But emptied himself" is a clear reference to Isaiah 53:12, "He poured out his soul." Here it includes both the Incarnation and the Atonement. "Taking the form of a servant" must refer to the Servant par excellence, who is Isaiah's Servant of the Lord. The reference is to the ministry of Jesus, which was that of the Servant Messiah. "Being born in the likeness of men," like the following clause "being found in human form," stresses the reality of the Incarnation. Despite his heavenly origin, nothing in his earthly appearance distinguished him from man. We are reminded of Isaiah's Servant:

> He had no form or comeliness that we should look at him,
> and no beauty that we should desire him (Isa. 53:2).

"He humbled himself" is reminiscent of Isaiah 53:7; and "unto death," of Isaiah 53:12. "Yes," comments Paul, "and a cross-death at that!"

"Therefore God has highly exalted him." This verse represents what the Greeks called the *peripeteia*, or turning point, in the drama. Obedience leads on to exaltation. The word "exalted" reminds us that it was prophesied of the Suffering Servant that he would be "exalted" (Isa. 52:13). Applied to Christ, the word includes the Resurrection and the Ascension. It is generally agreed that "the name which is above every name" is the name "*Kyrios*" in Greek, or "Lord." That it is the supreme name is shown by the fact that the men who made the Greek version of the Old Testament, the Septuagint, used this word *Kyrios* to render the ineffable name of God himself (Yahweh).

Verses 10 and 11 tell us why God exalted Jesus. It was that all created things wherever they exist—in heaven, on earth, or in the underworld—might do homage to the Lord Jesus, and every tongue join in uttering the words which comprised the earliest Christian creed: *Kyrios Jesus*—"Jesus is Lord." See Romans 10:9 and I Corinthians 12:3 for the same confession of faith.

Notice, too, that the phrases "every knee should bow" and "every tongue confess" come from Isaiah 45:23.

And with words which suggest the final purpose of the infinite God, "to the glory of God the Father," the hymn draws to a majestic liturgical close.

Work Out Your Own Salvation (2:12-18)

Paul now picks up his exhortation, which was interrupted by the Christ Hymn.

"Therefore, my beloved, as you have always obeyed, so now, not only as in my presence but much more in my absence, work out your own salvation with fear and trembling" (2:12). The last phrase means "seriously and reverently." But what is this? Is it possible that Paul, the champion of salvation by faith alone, advises his converts to secure it by works? No; only if we separate verse 12 from verse 13 will we draw this wrong conclusion. Paul is not thinking of works which a man must do in order to earn his salvation; he is concerned with the fruits of the Christian life which can appear only as God produces them in us. Equally, however, such fruits cannot appear if man resists God's work in his heart. Religious progress always depends on the grace of God; but without man's co-operation God himself is helpless. "For God is at work in you, both to will and to work for his good pleasure" (2:13). Paul insists that both the willing to do good and the putting of it into effect depend on the God who is busy working out his good and gracious purpose in us. Therefore "work out your own salvation" really means, not "Devote yourselves energetically to the saving of your own souls," but, "Co-operate with God in producing the fruits of the Christian life, which are love, joy, peace, and all the rest." Let them do this, and there will be no further need to worry about the little dissensions in their fellowship.

Paul continues (2:14) by warning them against "grumbling or questioning." He wants them to be "blameless and innocent, children of God without blemish in the midst of a crooked and perverse generation." These last words Moses had used of the children of Israel (Deut. 32:5). They are to "shine as lights in the world" (2:15), God's luminaries in a dark earth. We recall our Lord's words to his disciples, "You are the light of the world" (Matt. 5:14). And they are to hold fast "the word of life [the gospel], so that in the day of Christ [the day of his coming in glory] I may be proud that I did not run in vain or labor in vain." (2:16). Note Paul's metaphors. He pictures himself looking back from the Great Day and seeing that his apostolic labors in Philippi have not been wasted.

Then (2:17) he turns to contemplate the worst. "I am ready to die for you, if necessary," he means; "I rejoice at this, and I wish you to do the same." But his metaphor, which is derived from sacrifice, needs a little explaining. He says, "Even if I am to be poured as a libation upon the sacrificial offering of your faith, I am glad and rejoice with you all." Notice first that a "libation" is a cup of wine poured out as an offering to God, like David's draught of water from the well of Bethlehem (II Sam. 23:13-17). Paul pictures the Philippian Christians as priests offering up their "faith" (their Christian witness) to God, while he himself gives his life's blood as an accompanying sacrifice.

This grim prospect he surveys with the utmost cheerfulness. Assuming that they, too, rejoice in their sacrifice, he tells them that he shares in their joy. Then (2:18) he bids them take a like view of the double sacrifice. Let them rejoice in their own sacrifice, but let them share also his joy in his. There is a correspondence in sacrifice; let there also be a correspondence in joy. Was there ever a more indomitably joyful Christian?

PAUL'S PLANS
Philippians 2:19-30

Turning his thoughts to the future, Paul discusses his plans and inserts what are really two little letters of recommendation for Timothy and Epaphroditus.

"I hope in the Lord Jesus to send Timothy to you soon, so that I may be cheered by news of you" (2:19). All his hoping is done in union with his living Lord. Timothy, when he returns from his proposed visit, will, Paul hopes, bring cheering news from Philippi. But, as verse 23 shows, Paul does not yet know what news about himself, good or bad, Timothy will take with him. Timothy appears here as one of his trustiest supporters, with a gift for "caring," for Paul says, "I have no one like him, who will be genuinely anxious for your welfare" (2:20). The next verse (2:21) almost suggests that Paul, anxious to retain Timothy, had pressed others to go and had received only refusals. "They all look after their own interests, not those of Jesus

Christ," he comments bitterly. Is this an exaggerated charge?
Perhaps; but it is intelligible in one whose own devotion to Christ
was so complete. "But Timothy's worth you know," he continues
(2:22), using a Greek word which suggests metal which has
been tested and found genuine. Something of Timothy's sterling
qualities the Philippian Christians must have learned during his
first visit (Acts 16); and probably in the interval he had visited
Philippi yet again. Paul says, "You know . . . how as a son with
a father he has served with me in the gospel." What a very duti-
ful spiritual son Timothy must have been to deserve this tribute!
But Timothy is not the only guest they may expect in Philippi.
Though he is still unsure what the authorities will do with him,
Paul has a Christ-inspired confidence that he will find himself in
Philippi at no distant date. (Verse 23 is an argument for those
who think this epistle came from an Ephesian prison. If Paul is
writing from Rome, it is odd that he plans, on release, to go to
Macedonia and does not so much as mention his plan to go west,
which he declared in Romans 15:28. His hope of coming to
Philippi is also mentioned in Philippians 1:26.)

The next paragraph recommends Epaphroditus. Probably a
native of Philippi, he has a name which means "charming." And
what a charming character Paul gives him! This man, possibly
one of their local pastors, the Philippians had sent on a dual
errand—to take their present of money to Paul, and to stay with
the Apostle as long as he needed him. So devotedly had he
served Paul that he had fallen seriously ill. It was with distress
that the Philippians had heard of his illness, and that Epaphroditus
heard, in turn, of their dismay. When he recovered, he naturally
longed to be back among his own folk again, and Paul, observ-
ing this, decided to let him go home. In this letter which Epaphroditus probably carried with him when he went, Paul bespeaks
a cordial welcome for him.

"I have thought it necessary to send to you Epaphroditus my
brother and fellow worker and fellow soldier" (2:25). What a
noble description! Brother in the faith, fellow worker in the gospel, fellow soldier in the Christian conflict: theirs is a common
sympathy, a common work, and a common danger. But he is
more; he is "your messenger and minister to my need." The
phrase means "your messenger to meet my needs." The next
verse (2:26) explains why Paul is sending him at once: "he has
been longing for you all, and has been distressed because you

heard that he was ill." The heart of Epaphroditus was where his responsibility was. Paul realizes it and approves it. (Here again is a point in favor of the Ephesian theory discussed in the Introduction: not only has news of his illness reached Philippi, but news of their resultant distress has reached him, all of which may imply the nearness of Paul and the Philippians.)

"Indeed he was ill, near to death. But God had mercy on him" (2:27). Paul attributes Epaphroditus' recovery to God's mercy, and adds that, if he had died, his own troubles would have been increased; for the "sorrow upon sorrow" must mean the sorrow that would have been Paul's if his friend had died, plus the bitterness of his own imprisonment. The next sentence (2:28) may be better translated: "I am in the greater haste to send him." The reason follows: "That you may rejoice at seeing him again, and that I may be less anxious." One wonders if the worth of Epaphroditus was not properly appreciated at Philippi, for Paul proceeds: "So receive him in the Lord"—give him a real Christian welcome—"and honor such men" (2:29). Even in our churches today it is not always the best Christians who are most highly esteemed. Our estimates of men are apt to be affected by things like money and prestige. Paul's reason for valuing Epaphroditus so highly comes out vividly in the last verse of the chapter: "For he nearly died for the work of Christ, risking his life to complete your service to me" (2:30). "Risking" translates a Greek word which means "he gambled with his life." Certain laymen in the Early Church who risked their lives to nurse cases of plague and fever were known as the "Gamblers," their name deriving from the Greek word describing Epaphroditus. "I am God's gambler," says Kagawa, "I have staked my life on him." God send the Church more gamblers like Epaphroditus and Kagawa!

PAUL'S APOLOGIA
Philippians 3:1-21

Warning Against Judaizers (3:1-3)

The word "finally" seems to suggest that Paul was drawing his letter to a close. But a last warning against the Judaizers leads him into a moving personal apologia. "Rejoice in the Lord" (3:1) picks up the thought of 2:18, as it sounds the keynote of this letter. Christians are to be joyful, but theirs must be the joy that springs from Christ and communion with him. But what do the following words mean? "To write the same things to you is not irksome to me, and is safe for you." Is Paul justifying his repetition of the command to rejoice? Or is he referring to a warning which he had given in some previous letter? (The Early Church Father, Polycarp, talks about Paul's "letters" to the Philippians.) We cannot tell. In any case, like any good teacher, Paul is not ashamed of repeating himself. Dr. Johnson once said that men need to be *reminded* far more than they need to be informed.

Now comes the warning: "Look out for the dogs, look out for the evil-workers, look out for those who mutilate the flesh" (3:2). These are Paul's old enemies, the Judaizers, the men who argued that to become a perfect Christian, one must add circumcision and keeping of the Law to simple faith in Christ. "Dogs" is a strong word. Did Paul use it because the Judaizers fed on the garbage of carnal ordinances? All these men are interested in is "incision"—laceration of the flesh: a scornful name for circumcision. What a caricature of the true Israel! On the contrary, Paul says, "we are the true circumcision, who worship God in spirit, and glory in Christ Jesus, and put no confidence in the flesh" (3:3). Because we believe in spiritual and not in physical marks, we are "the true circumcision," the real Israel of God, the Israel which, rejecting all trust in outward privilege (literally "the flesh"), worships God in spirit (see John 4:24), and exults in Christ as Savior.

Retrospect and Prospect (3:4-16)

First (3:5), Paul lists his inherited Jewish privileges, almost as if he were counting them off on his fingers: "circumcised on the eighth day"—the day prescribed in the Law for the native-born Jew (Gen. 17:12; Lev. 12:3); "of the people of Israel"—from the original stock, "Israel" being the name for the covenanted people of God; "of the tribe of Benjamin"—belonging to a tribe second in honor only to Judah, like our saying, "of Norman blood" or "descended from the Pilgrim Fathers"; "a Hebrew born of Hebrews"—the son of parents who spoke Hebrew (Aramaic).

Next (3:5-6), he records his Jewish attainments: "as to the law a Pharisee"—that is, belonging to the strictest sect in Jewry;

"as to zeal a persecutor of the church"—true words full of sad irony (see Gal. 1:13 and I Cor. 15:9); "as to righteousness under the law blameless"—we think of the rich young ruler in the Gospels who said, "All these I have observed from my youth" (Mark 10:20). But note that Paul was "blameless" only from the Pharisaic standpoint. The word is far from meaning "sinless," as Romans 7:7-24 shows.

Such were his privileges as a Pharisee. Now (3:7-11) he tells us what he gained when he met Christ. These proud privileges proved worse than useless; when he found Christ, he counted them a dead loss. Indeed (3:8), compared with "the surpassing worth of knowing Christ," absolutely everything can be called a loss, so highly does he rate "the unsearchable riches of Christ" (Eph. 3:8). Knowledge of Christ does not mean here intellectual apprehension, but rather personal appropriation of Christ and communion with him. How impressive, too, is Paul's description of the Savior: "Christ Jesus my Lord"!

Indeed, Paul has actually "suffered the loss of all things" for Christ's sake. Is there no pang of regret? On the contrary, he counts them as refuse—the scraps thrown to the dogs—if only he may "gain Christ."

Verse 9 explains what it is to "gain Christ." First, it means being "found" in Christ—being united to him by the closest of bonds. This he further elucidates: "Not having a righteousness of my own, based on law, but that which is through faith in Christ, the righteousness from God that depends on faith." Here is the doctrine of justification by faith which bulks so large in Galatians and Romans. Let us dwell on it for a moment.

It is the heart's desire of every religious man to "get right" with God. But how? There is a choice of ways: law-righteousness *or* faith-righteousness. As a practicing Pharisee, Paul tried the first of these, believing that by doing the works prescribed by the Law of Moses he could put himself right with God and find peace. (We think of the Pharisee in Christ's parable who thought he could earn God's favor by all the meritorious things he did.) But Paul found by bitter experience that this way does not work. It leads only to failure and despair. Then he met Christ—and found the true answer. To get right with God you must give up all hope of earning your salvation by laying up a credit balance of good deeds in the ledgers of heaven. Instead you must confess yourself a sinner and cast yourself on God's

mercy offered to you in Christ, who by God's appointing has
died to save you from your sins. When you do this, God accepts
you for Christ's sake, forgives you, sets you among his people
(the Church), and you are on the way to salvation. As the first
kind of righteousness was a law-righteousness ("a righteousness
of my own," Paul calls it, since it was to be achieved by one's
own efforts), so the second and true righteousness comes "from
God" and "depends on faith," that is, on man's unreserved response to God's gracious dealing with him in Christ.

Verse 10 expounds more fully what is involved in gaining
Christ. It means knowing Christ and "the power of his resurrection." "Know" has the sense of "experience." It means experi-
encing Christ's power, the power of the risen Lord, energizing
your whole inner life, so that you can conquer the old enemy,
the "flesh" (Rom. 7:24-25), and have the glad assurance of immortality (Rom. 8:11). But there is another side to "knowing
Christ." It means also sharing his sufferings. Paul is not thinking of martyrdom, but of a man's dying with Christ to his old
bad life (see Rom. 6:4-8). Before you can "rise with Christ"
into newness of life (see Col. 3:1), you must undergo an experience analogous to Christ's crucifixion, a dying to sin. This is
what Paul means in verse 10 by "becoming like him in his
death."

Finally (3:11), Paul looks away to the ultimate goal of this
experience: "that if possible I may attain the resurrection from the
dead." This is the triumphant consummation in the glory of another world of the Christian life lived in Christ here below.

Paul, however, admits (3:12) that he is fully aware of his
own imperfection, and goes on to bid the "mature" among them
to imitate him in pressing forward in the Christian life. Probably
in these words he is administering a gentle rebuke to some of
his readers who were prone to imagine that they were already
"perfect." "Not that I have already obtained this or am already
perfect," he comments. "This" must mean his knowledge of
Christ. "But I press on to make it my own, because Christ Jesus
has made me his own." The Greek verb here translated "make
my own" means to "lay hold of," "arrest," or "appropriate."
Christ had "arrested" Paul on the Damascus Road with a specific
purpose: so that Paul might get to know Christ and serve him.
We may judge that Christ's purpose for Paul had already largely
been fulfilled; but the Apostle feels that there is still much to be

achieved in the way of knowing and serving his Lord. Hence he says: "I do not consider that I have made it my own; but one thing I do, forgetting what lies behind and straining forward to what lies ahead, I press on toward the goal for the prize of the upward call of God in Christ Jesus" (3:13-14). Paul's metaphor is drawn from the foot race. Note the apostolic single-mindedness expressed in "but one thing." But what is it which "lies behind"? He must refer to his past achievements in the Christian life. The secret of Christian progress is to forget one's past accomplishments and go on to new ones. How vividly the participle "straining forward" suggests the runner going flat out for the tape! And ever his eye is on "the goal" with its prize in store. Paul must be thinking of final Christian perfection and its heavenly reward. The prize is not that which consists in God's call but that to which God calls—the reward of his obedience to that call.

Then Paul applies what he has been saying. "Let those of us who are mature be thus minded" (3:15). In other words, the only true maturity is to be always pressing on to it. For does not Christian perfection consist in the striving after the goal? "And if in anything you are otherwise minded, God will reveal that also to you." Paul is thinking of the "perfectionists" again. If they do not yet see eye to eye with him, God may be trusted to show them their mistake. Paul is very sure that he possesses God's truth.

The closing verse of this section (3:16) means literally: "Only, whereunto we have arrived, by the same let us guide our steps." This must mean that we are to guide our steps by such truth as we have already reached. Fidelity to truth already acquired is the condition of getting more from God.

Beware of Libertines (3:17-21)

Now Paul returns to his exhortation. "Brethren, join in imitating me" (3:17; see I Cor. 4:16; 11:1). Again how sure Paul must have been that he had "the mind of Christ" to talk in this way! (I Cor. 2:16). "And mark those who so live as you have an example in us." "Us" means Paul, Timothy, and Epaphroditus. The men to be "marked" are certain church leaders in Philippi who follow Paul's lead. The rest of the Christians in Philippi could profitably copy them. For, unfortunately, many live, whom he has often mentioned and now does so with tears, as "enemies of the cross of Christ" (3:18). These are not men who rejected the doctrine of the Atonement; they are men whose lives gave the lie to the spirit of the Cross, lovers of self-indulgence, not of self-denial. Neither the Judaizers nor the "perfectionists" seem to be in Paul's mind. Everything he says of these people points to their having been Christian libertines—people, possibly Gentiles, who turned their Christian liberty into unchristian license.

"Their god," Paul says, "is the belly" (3:19). In those days "the belly" covered other vices besides gluttony, including sexual sins. "They glory in their shame" means that they boast of what is a disgrace to them; but "their end is destruction."

How different from us whose hopes are set other-where! "But our commonwealth is in heaven" (3:20). "Commonwealth" would be better rendered as "capital city." So Philo uses the word, and the context here seems to demand this meaning. Philippi was a Roman colony (Acts 16:12)—a miniature Rome in distant Macedonia—in which Roman veterans had been settled and which enjoyed rights and customs like Rome's own. We know from Acts 16:21 that the Roman legionaries in Philippi took pride in this Roman citizenship and all its privileges. All this provides the background to Paul's words: "But our true capital city is in heaven: here on earth we are a colony of this heavenly city where our Lord resides and from which we eagerly expect him to come as Savior."

This Savior, Paul says, "will change our lowly body to be like his glorious body" (3:21). Here is the great doctrine of I Corinthians 15:35-57 in brief. "Our lowly body" is the body, subject to decay and death, belonging to our mortal state. When Christ comes in his glory, he will transform it so that it resembles "the body of his glory" (the literal meaning of the Greek)—that body, clad in the splendor of another world, in which Paul had seen Christ on the Damascus Road. Paul's doctrine of the next life, be it noted, is neither the Greek doctrine of the immortality of the soul nor the Pharisaic one of the resurrection of the flesh. What he expects hereafter is "a spiritual body"—an organism created by God's Spirit, suitable to the needs of the heavenly world, as our present body, made of flesh, is suitable to the needs of this one. Such a transformation of our present lowly body will be in keeping with the Savior's mighty power: "by the power which enables him even to subject all things to himself" (3:21). The phrase, echoing Psalm 8:6, recalls the great affirmation of I Corinthians 15:25: "For he must reign until he has put all his enemies under his feet," of which enemies the last to be put down is death.

FINAL ADMONITIONS
Philippians 4:1-9

First comes an exhortation to "stand firm," addressed to his beloved converts whom he calls "my joy and crown" (compare I Thess. 2:19). The crown, or garland, was the reward of the victorious athlete at the Greek games.

At this point Paul seems to have remembered something Epaphroditus had reported from Philippi. Two Christian women, Euodia and Syntyche ("Fragrance" and "Felicity"?), had disagreed in some way. We know nothing about them beyond the fact that they had quarreled. What a grim thought! Paul begs them to "agree in the Lord" (4:2). Let them only realize their common bond to Christ, and reconciliation will not be far away. But the intervention of a third party may also help (4:3). Who the "true yokefellow" is, remains an unsolved mystery. It may have been Epaphroditus, the bearer of the letter. On the other hand the Greek, which means "joiner-together," may have been a proper name. In that case Paul was punning on it, "True reconciler, fulfill the promise of your name!" "Help these women," Paul counsels him, "for they have labored side by side with me in the gospel." There is nothing sadder than to see two good Christian people fall out. We cannot identify the Clement who had been one of their fellow workers "whose names are in the book of life." The phrase suggests that they had died. Occurring half a dozen times in Revelation, "the book of life" signifies the heavenly register of God's people (see Luke 10:20). Men may forget, but God remembers his faithful servants and lists them as his own.

With verse 4 Paul returns to his favorite theme: "Rejoice in the Lord always; again I will say, Rejoice." The repetition must be designed to convince any who might doubt that joy can accompany afflictions. "Let all men know your forbearance," he advises in verse 5. The Greek word here is Matthew Arnold's "sweet reasonableness." The Greeks said it was justice and something better. It describes the man who knows when to relax justice and let mercy come breaking in. But what is the force of the following "The Lord is at hand"? It is generally taken to mean, "Christ is coming back soon." But, since Paul proceeds to talk about prayer, it may well be an echo of Psalm 145:18, "The LORD is near to all who call upon him."

"Have no anxiety about anything" (4:6) is Christ's own warning against worry (Matt. 6:25; Luke 12:22). What follows reads like a practical comment on it, which says in effect: "True prayer and anxious care cannot coexist: the way to be anxious about nothing is to be prayerful about everything." The word "prayer" represents our general approach to God in prayer; "supplication," the cry of personal need. With these, when we let our "requests be made known to God," should go "thanksgiving." If they pray in this way, Paul promises (4:7), "the peace of God, which passes all understanding"—transcends all our comprehension—"will keep" (literally "garrison") their "hearts" and "minds." He ends with the phrase "in Christ Jesus," as though to say, "Outside him there is no safety."

The paragraph began with joy; it ends with peace. Is Paul saying that if we have not God's peace in our hearts we cannot have his song on our lips?

The first verse of the next brief paragraph (4:8-9) is unique in Paul: unique not only because it contains words not found elsewhere in his letters—or indeed in the whole New Testament—but also because the virtues it commends are those of Greek moral philosophy. Note the stress on what is "true" and "just," on what is attractive and high-toned, but, above all, commendation of "excellence" and what is "worthy of praise." Why did Paul urge his readers to "think about" or take into account such ethical values? Probably the Christians in Philippi, under stress of persecution, were tending to be blind to what was good in the pagan life all around them. They may even have asked Paul what attitude they should adopt to such pagan moral ideals. This verse gives us Paul's answer and it is worthy of him: "Take account of good," he is saying, "wherever you find it." Consider the words one by one. "True" includes both speech and fact. "Honorable" is Matthew Arnold's "nobly serious." "Just" stands for all that accords with the highest conceptions of what is right. "Pure" has all the width of our "pure" in its ethical sense. "Lovely" means what is "attractive" or "winsome." "Gracious" is literally "fair-sounding" and so "high-toned." "Excellence," a word not found elsewhere in Paul, is one of the great terms of pagan ethics, with all the nuances of our "good." "Worthy of praise" contains the idea of moral approbation and so "merit." "Think about these things" would, however, be better rendered "take these things into account."

Then Paul turns from pagan morals to his own teaching (4:9) —"What you have learned and received and heard and seen in me, do." The first two verbs describe Paul's own teaching; the second two, his personal example. If the Philippians do this, "the God of peace," the God who is the Author and Source of peace, a favorite description of God in Paul, will be with them (see Rom. 15:33; 16:20; II Cor. 13:11; and I Thess. 5:23).

THE PRESENT FROM PHILIPPI
Philippians 4:10-20

Very delicately Paul now says "Thank you" for the gift from Philippi which had occasioned the letter. First, he hints that he could have managed without the money, since he has learned the secret of true Christian independence (4:11-13); and then he thanks them for their gift, declaring it to be a token of true Christian fellowship and an offering which God approves (4:14-18).

"I rejoice in the Lord greatly that now at length you have revived your concern for me" (4:10). They had always been concerned for him—witness their original financial help to him in Thessalonica (4:16)—but circumstances had prevented them from showing it practically. "You were indeed concerned for me, but you had no opportunity," he says.

Then he asserts his "independence": "Not that I complain of want; for I have learned, in whatever state I am, to be content" (4:11). Note the word "content." Its Greek equivalent was a word used by the Stoics to describe the man who was sufficient unto himself in all circumstances. The Stoic was *self*-sufficient; Paul, as we shall see, was *Christ*-sufficient.

Verse 12 explains. Poverty or plenty makes no difference to Paul, for he has "learned the secret" of facing both with equanimity. "Learned the secret" is literally "been initiated into," a term popularized by the Greek mystery religions. Here it is used in a quite general sense.

Then (4:13) he lets us into the secret: "I can do all things in him who strengthens me." "In union with Christ," Paul means, "who infuses his power into me, I am able for anything." The secret of his "independence" is dependence on Another! How many Christians since Paul have learned the same secret! From this text, as he died, Oliver Cromwell drew his comfort.

At 4:14 Paul returns to the kindness of the Philippians. "It was kind of you to share my trouble," he says, meaning by this not simply their gift of money but their practical sympathy illustrated by their sending of Epaphroditus. Indeed, they had done something which none of his other churches had done: from "the beginning of the gospel" (that is, when it was first preached in Macedonia), Philippi alone among his churches "had gone shares with him in the matter of debit and credit." We have retranslated the Greek in order to show its commercial style. What Paul means is: "No church but yourselves had any financial dealings with me." "For even in Thessalonica you sent me help once and again" (4:16). During his second missionary journey Paul had gone on to Thessalonica from Philippi (Acts 17:1); and during his time in Thessalonica at least two gifts had reached him from Philippi.

Now (4:17) comes Paul's final avowal of his independence. "Not that I seek the gift" ("It's not your money I am after"); "but I seek the fruit which increases to your credit." A bolder rendering of the Greek would again show the commercial flavor of the sentence: "I seek the interest that is accumulating to your credit." Where? In the ledgers of heaven.

Paul continues (4:18): "I have received full payment, and more." "Received" is the customary formula of receipt, often found in the Egyptian papyri. "Paid in full I am," Paul says, "and more than that." He is referring to the gifts Epaphroditus had brought from Philippi. But they are more than a mere human gift; they are "a fragrant offering, a sacrifice acceptable and pleasing to God." The language of business gives place to that of worship. "Fragrant offering" is a common Old Testament expression for the sacrifice whose fragrance is supposed to be well pleasing to Deity. Does Paul's language sound a trifle fulsome? Then let us remember that the early Christians regarded a gift to an Apostle as a gift to God whose envoy he was. "This gift of yours," Paul says, "pleases God, and the God who values it will not forget the givers." "And my God will supply every need of yours according to his riches in glory in Christ Jesus" (4:19).

"In glory" means either "gloriously" or "in God's glorious presence." With a doxology the section ends.

GREETINGS AND BENEDICTION
Philippians 4:21-23

"Greet every saint in Christ Jesus" (4:21) means, "My Christian greetings to every one of God's people," for the words "in Christ Jesus" go, as in Romans 16:22 and I Corinthians 16:19, with the verb. "All the saints greet you, especially those of Caesar's household" (4:22). We know what kind of people formed "Caesar's household": they were Imperial servants, some slaves, some freedmen—a sort of Imperial Civil Service. But we cannot be sure where these saints served. At one time, this verse and 1:13 were thought to tie this letter to Rome. Since we now know from inscriptions that these Imperial servants were found all over the Roman Empire, we cannot be so certain. If they were domiciled in Rome, they must have belonged to the "establishment" of Nero's palace. But they may have lived in Ephesus where, as some think, this letter was written.

With a simple benediction invoking on his readers Christ's grace—his wonderful kindness to sinners—"the Epistle Radiant with Joy" comes to an end.

THE LETTER OF PAUL TO THE

COLOSSIANS

INTRODUCTION

Colossae

Where is Colossae? Or, rather, since not a stone of it now stands, where *was* it? If you locate Ephesus on a map of the Roman province of Asia in Paul's time, and then let your eyes travel about a hundred miles due east, you will see three cities—Laodicea, Hierapolis, and Colossae—all lying in the valley of the River Lycus, and practically within sight of each other. Hierapolis and Laodicea, both mentioned in our letter (Col. 4:13), stood on either side of the valley, with the Lycus between. About a dozen miles up the river, and straddling it, lay Colossae, to which Paul sent his letter.

The Lycus Valley was noted for three things: earthquakes, chalk deposits, and wealth. From the first of these Laodicea, which has given our language a colorful epithet for "lukewarm" (see Rev. 3:14-16), suffered very severely in A.D. 60. The chalk deposits covered everything like a stone shroud, but also fertilized the surrounding pasturages. The wealth of the region was famous. Rich grazings for sheep, a prosperous woolen industry in consequence, and a fine dyeing trade all conspired to make the people wealthy and to produce a complacent prosperity which John, the Seer of Revelation, later deplored (Rev. 3:17).

Through the years Laodicea had grown into the political and financial head of the area; Hierapolis had become an important center of trade and a well-known resort. Only Colossae had failed to match the commercial prosperity of its neighbors. It was perhaps the least important town to which Paul ever wrote.

To complete the picture, we should remember that the region had a big Jewish population. The first Jews to make their homes in the Lycus Valley had been deported there, many years before, from Babylon and Mesopotamia, by Antiochus the Great of Syria. As these had prospered, others of their fellow countrymen had come to share their prosperity. Indeed, we know that in 62

B.C. so much Jewish money was being sent from the Lycus Valley to Jerusalem to pay the Temple tax that the Roman governor of the area felt compelled to put an embargo on the export of currency from the province.

With this picture of Colossae and its neighborhood in our minds, we are now ready to consider Paul's contacts and correspondence with it.

Paul and Colossae

But did Paul really write the Letter to the Colossians? There was a time when his authorship was seriously questioned. Students found words in his letter not to be found in his other letters; they found a conception of Christ's Person which seemed to them higher than anything discoverable elsewhere in his writings. Therefore, they said, Paul could not have written it. Neither of these objections has really any weight. The special circumstances which called forth the letter easily explain the new words, as they explain also the soaring claims made for Christ in the letter. The heresy which had arisen in the Colossian Church compelled Paul to think out the implications of his doctrine of Christ and to explain them in cosmic terms. In short, though a few still deny the letter to Paul, there is nothing in it which need make us hesitate for a moment in pronouncing it Paul's.

When Paul wrote to the Colossians, he had never visited Colossae (Col. 2:1). How, then, did he first establish Christian contact with the Lycus Valley?

The answer is that he made such contact during his third missionary journey (A.D. 53-56), when he evangelized Ephesus and its surrounding regions. (The reader here should look up the historical narrative relating to this journey given us by Luke in Acts 18 and 19.) At this time Paul spent no less than three years in and around Ephesus, and it would be true to say that in Ephesus he founded a diocese, or group of churches, rather than a congregation. Doubtless it was during his Ephesian ministry that men from the Lycus Valley, visiting Ephesus, heard the gospel for the first time, accepted it, and on returning home founded the three churches in Laodicea, Hierapolis, and Colossae. One such was Epaphras (Col. 1:7; 4:12). Converted, perhaps by Paul in Ephesus, he had gone back to his native Colossae and founded the church there.

What kind of church was it? Though it must have included Jews, we gather from the letter that it was predominantly Gentile. "Estranged and hostile in mind" (1:21) is the way Paul describes the Colossians' former spiritual state, and it suggests that of Gentiles. So, too, when he speaks (1:27) of making known the mystery of Christ among the Gentiles, we are tolerably sure he has the Christians in Colossae primarily in his mind. Finally, the sins enumerated in 3:5-7 are regarded as characteristically Gentile sins.

The Occasion, Date, and Source of the Letter

How did Paul come to write this letter?

When Epaphras and his friends had first evangelized Colossae, they had preached the gospel in all its Pauline purity. But very soon things had begun to happen in Colossae which threatened that purity and called forth Paul's letter. Some of the new converts showed a strong disposition to embellish the simple gospel with all manner of fancy additions from their own fashionable cults and religious philosophies. No doubt it was Epaphras who first brought news of the trouble to Paul's prison. We are not to assume that all was black on the horizon in Colossae; for Paul in his letter finds reason to praise the Colossians' faith and love (1:4) and to congratulate them on their firm Christian stand (2:5). But certain sinister tendencies were appearing in the Colossian church which, if allowed to develop, would ruin all. To meet this danger Paul wrote his letter.

But where did he write it and when?

The traditional answers to these questions are: in Rome, about A.D. 61 or 62. We think they are the right answers. But in recent years a number of interpreters have suggested that the prison from which Paul wrote was not in Rome but in Ephesus, and that one or all of the so-called "Prison Epistles"—Colossians, Ephesians, Philippians, and Philemon—were written there. If so, they would date from the time when Paul was in Ephesus, that is, about A.D. 54-55. On the question whether Paul was ever imprisoned in Ephesus, we must refer the reader to the Introduction to Philippians. There is no very convincing direct evidence for such an imprisonment, though there is some circumstantial. In the case of Philippians we have tried to leave the issue open, arguing that, if we could be sure Paul was imprisoned in Ephesus, then some details in Philippians would agree with this very well. But there is one fact which, as it seems, links Colossians and Philemon with Rome. We know that Luke was with Paul when he wrote these two letters (Col. 4:14; Philemon 24), and Luke was with Paul in Rome, since the last "we-passage" in Acts brings Paul and Luke to Rome. "When we came into Rome," says Acts 28:16, certainly implying the presence of the author. But the narrative describing Paul's Ephesian ministry in Acts 18 and 19 is not among the "we-passages," and we therefore surmise that Luke was not there. For this reason and because it is generally better to follow tradition than to embrace an unproved speculation, we assign Colossians to Rome and date it about A.D. 61.

The Colossian Heresy

The nature of the heresy in Colossae should be considered for a full understanding of the letter. To discover what precisely it was, we have to piece together the clues in the letter itself.

From what Paul says, we gather that this heresy threatened the supremacy of Christ for faith, trafficked in astrology, demonology, and asceticism, and stressed ritual and holy days, circumcision, and worship of angels. What does all this add up to? Something Jewish, or something pagan? The answer is: an amalgam of both, with of course a Christian basis.

The mention of new moons, festivals, sabbaths, angels, and circumcision (Col. 2:11,16,18) strongly suggests that the heresy had Jewish elements. But, equally strongly, the allusions to a specious "philosophy," to "elemental spirits of the universe" (2:8, 20); to asceticism (2:23); and to an inadequate conception of Christ's Person (1:15-20; 2:15) suggest that the heresy had a deep "Gnostic" tincture. Gnosticism (from a Greek word meaning "knowledge") represented the pagan "Higher Thought" of the time. It took many shapes and forms; but one root principle of it, held by all Gnostics, or "Knowing Ones" (shall we say "The Intellectuals"?), was that *matter was evil* and the creation so badly flawed that the high God could have no direct communication with it. If man, tied to his body of flesh, was ever to know the transcendent God and find salvation, there must be some kind of spiritual ladder to be climbed, some sort of lore to be learned, enabling him to leave the material world behind and make contact with the unapproachable God. So the Gnostics conceived of a whole hierarchy or collection of spiritual beings (often called "aeons") or mediators, strung out between God and this evil world. By their help and by the knowledge of secret lore and passwords a man might hope to win through to the higher world. Some kind of religious philosophy like this seems to have flourished in Colossae. It was a system in which Christ apparently had a high, but not the supreme, place. What kind of morals went along with it? If you believe that matter, and therefore the body, is evil, you may take one of two ways. Either you keep your body in severe check by a rigorous asceticism, or you take the line that, since the body is evil, it does not much matter what you do. Gnosticism could thus issue in either asceticism or immorality.

From all this it follows that the heretics in Colossae were propagating two serious errors. On the one hand, they were dethroning Christ from his unique place as the only true mediator between God and men. On the other, they were forcing on the Christians in Colossae an unhealthy asceticism which was mixed up with Jewish taboos and Jewish observance of new moons and holy days. In chapter 1, verses 15-23, Paul is obviously attacking the first, that is, the Christological error. Just as obviously in chapter 2, verses 8-23, he is warning his readers against the second error, the ethical aberrations of the heretics.

The Meaning and Message of Colossians

How much good doctrine heretics have been responsible for, indirectly! Not the least of these were the nameless ones in Colossae who set Paul thinking out his doctrine of Christ in such terms that he found he had to give his Lord the freedom of the universe. The Christ of Colossians is the Cosmic Christ. Not that the heretics had any design or dream of effecting this. They were evidently aiming at a "superior" Christianity of their own. Finding the gospel too simple, they set out to embellish it with this or that element of "philosophy" (though Paul has a much blunter name for it, "empty deceit") and ritual. In fact, as Paul saw, they were scaling down the Person and work of Christ, limiting the scope of his redemptive work, filching from him his uniqueness. For this there could be but one remedy—to make clear who Christ really is and what he has really done for men.

So Paul says in reply to them: Christ is not one in a system of mediators. He is the principle and goal of creation: the visible manifestation of the unseen God, the Father's First-born, his Agent in creation, the totality of Deity corporately, the Head of the new Divine Community, the Reconciler of estranged men, God's great Secret now unveiled and containing in himself all the treasures of wisdom and knowledge (1:15—2:3).

What has Christ done? He has redeemed us: by the sacrifice of the Cross he has brought reconciliation, canceled the Law's indictment that stood against us, and triumphed over the demonic forces of evil (2:13-15).

No one who realizes the sufficiency of Christ's Saviorhood should bother any more with fads about foods or holy days, with angel-worship or visionary lore or any petty prohibitions about external things. These are only the shadows; the substance belongs to Christ (2:16-23).

From there Paul goes on to sketch the new life in Christ. "If then you have been raised with Christ, seek the things that are above" (3:1). This involves "killing" our old bad habits, telling the truth, showing forgiveness, building up Christian homes, and dealing graciously with outsiders (3:1—4:6).

We may ask, What has the letter to say to us today? This, first: To all who would "improve" Christianity by admixing it with spiritualism or Sabbatarianism or occultism or any such extra, it utters its warning: "What Christ is and has done for us is enough for salvation. We need no extra mediators, or taboos, or ascetics. To piece out the gospel with the rags and tatters of alien cults is not to enrich but to corrupt it."

And this, second: If the titles and place Paul assigns to Christ in Colossians surprise, and even stagger, us, they do but say what any true doctrine of Christ must say, that the Fact of Christ must somehow be embedded in creation, that all creation exists with him in view, and that in some deep mysterious way it has promise of Christ in it.

OUTLINE

COMMENTARY

ADDRESS AND THANKSGIVING
Colossians 1:1-14

Opening Salutation (1:1-2)

The way to begin a letter in Paul's day, as we have already explained, was: "A to B sends greeting." Paul follows the pattern in Colossians but expands it and links Timothy with himself as joint author, although Timothy may have done no more than approve the terms of the letter. Paul calls himself Christ's Apostle —his "Special Messenger"—"by the will of God," alluding no doubt to the day when the Risen Christ met him on the Damascus Road and changed the whole current of his life. Timothy was a native of Lystra, the son of a Greek father and a Jewish mother, who had probably become a Christian during the first journey of Paul and Barnabas through South Galatia (Acts 14:6-20). He joined Paul on the latter's second missionary journey (Acts 16: 1-5) and remained his right-hand man to the end.

The addressees are "the saints and faithful brethren in Christ at Colossae" (1:2). On "Colossae," see the Introduction. The root meaning of "saints" in the New Testament is "set apart" or "dedicated" to God. By "saints" *we* usually mean people who have, so to speak, achieved the ultimate in the spiritual life; but in the New Testament the primary stress is on their dedication to God rather than on any shining excellence of character. "Brethren," which means "fellow Christians," emphasizes the fact that they all belong together as members in God's great family, the Church. But this brotherhood, dedicated and loyal to God, is further described as "in Christ." This most famous of all Paul's phrases carries the sense not only of being "in communion with Christ" but of being "in the community of Christ"; for the divine act which sets a man "in Christ"—that is, makes him Christ's man, united to him by faith—sets him also in the society of Christ, which is the Church. The New Testament, we need always to remember, knows nothing of solitary religion or unattached Christians.

For his readers Paul prays "grace" and "peace from God our Father." As he does in the opening of Galatians, Ephesians, and Philippians, Paul here turns the usual pagan salutation "Cheerio"

to "Grace," that favorite word of Paul's to describe the wonderful kindness of God to sinners in Christ. "Peace" no doubt is the
usual oriental greeting, but who can doubt that on Paul's lips the
word was no conventional greeting, any more than it was on
Christ's (John 14:27). Rather, it was a fervent wish that his
readers would truly know that peace "with God" which is the
possession of all who have been forgiven by God for Christ's
sake. Only here, notice, does the name of the Father stand alone
in the opening salutation. Usually Paul says "from God the
Father and the Lord Jesus Christ."

Faith, Hope, and Love (1:3-8)

After the opening salutation it was usual, in an ancient letter,
to add a few conventional words of thanks for the welfare of the
persons addressed. Paul, too, likes to start with a thanksgiving,
though it is always a Christian and not merely a conventional
one. (The exception to the rule is of course Galatians, where
Paul found nothing in the situation for which to give thanks to
God.) The thanksgiving in Colossians, addressed to "God, the
Father of our Lord Jesus Christ"—that is, the God whom Jesus
Christ has revealed to us as Father—is woven around three short
but very important words, "faith," "love," and "hope." We are all
familiar with this triad from I Corinthians 13:13: "So faith,
hope, love abide." But it crops up so often in Paul's letters (Rom.
5:1-5; Eph. 4:2-5; Gal. 5:5-6; I Thess. 1:3; 5:8) that obviously
it summed up for him in three words the essence of the Christian
life. (We find the triad also in Hebrews 6:10-12; I Peter 1:3-8,
as well as in passages of the Apostolic Fathers, so that it may
have been a common early Christian way of describing, in a nut-
shell, the Christian life. Did it perhaps begin with an uncanonical
word of Jesus himself preserved for us by the Early Church
Father Macarius: "Take care of faith and hope through which
is begotten the love of God and of man which gives eternal
life"?)

Let us examine the constituent elements of this triad. "Faith"
describes Christianity on its religious side; it is the utter trust of
the sinner in his Savior who has died to redeem him. Love, *agape*,
whose best English equivalent is perhaps "caring," describes it
on its ethical side. But notice, these two, faith and love, may no
more be separated than the two sides of a coin; for faith, unless
it is a sham and a husk, "works through love" (Gal. 5:6) and

without it is completely worthless (I Cor. 13:2). This life of faith and love is, in turn, grounded on "hope," the word describing here not so much the act of hoping but the thing hoped for, which is the heavenly destiny God has "laid up" (as one would "store up" grain in a granary) for his saints hereafter.

Observe how the three members of the triad are delimited. Faith is faith in "Christ Jesus," the preposition denoting the *sphere* of their believing rather than the object of their faith. Their love is that which they "have for all the saints," that is, all their fellow Christians, the stress falling on the horizontal relationship of love which is, or ought to be, their practical response to the vertical one, the down-descending love of God to them in Christ. "Beloved, if God so loved us, we also ought to love one another" (I John 4:11). And their "hope," grounded on their faith and love, is that promised blessing which is stored like a treasure in God's heavenly treasure house. We recall the similar words of Peter, where the "living hope," founded on Christ's resurrection, is fixed on "an inheritance which is imperishable, undefiled, and unfading, kept in heaven for you" (I Peter 1:3-4). Does all this strike an otherworldly note which jars rudely on the this-worldliness of our contemporary civilization? Then let us remember two things: First, any true Christianity must strike both notes, and any account of the Faith which forgets that "here we have no lasting city" (Heb. 13:14) represents a grave falling away from the Christianity of the New Testament. Second: Paul's doctrine is not a mere "pie in the sky" otherworldliness, since, in his view, the hope laid up in heaven ought to be the most potent of incentives to Christian living here and now. As John put it, Christian hope is a sanctifying virtue (I John 3:3).

Of all this the Colossians have "heard before in the word of the truth, the gospel" (1:5). "Before" probably means, "before the heretics began unsettling you with their false doctrines." The gospel is defined as "the truth," "the true message" (as distinct from all heretical perversions) or, possibly, "the message about the truth." Not only have the Colossians heard it and made it their own, discerning in it the true grace of God, but it keeps "bearing fruit and growing" in the whole world (1:6). Here are two marks of the true gospel as distinct from all perversions of it: power to fructify—that is, in terms of human beings, to take and remake sinful men and women; and catholicity—Paul is probably contrasting the universality of the true gospel with the merely local range of the false gospel being propagated in Colossae.

Their knowledge of the gospel the Colossians owe to "Epaphras," who had evangelized Colossae under Paul's direction and whom Paul calls "our beloved fellow servant," or "slave"; that is, our partner in that voluntary bondage to Christ, to serve whom is the only true freedom. It was Epaphras who had told Paul in prison of the Colossians' "love in the Spirit" (1:8). Some would print "spirit" with a small letter, as referring to the human spirit of Paul's readers. We take the Revised Standard Version to be right in thinking of their love as inspired by the Holy Spirit, which is "the life of God in the soul of man," making Christians aware of God's love to them (Rom. 5:5) and prompting them in turn to love the brethren. Does not Paul set love first among the fruits of the Spirit (Gal. 5:22) and declare it the greatest of all spiritual gifts? (I Cor. 13).

A Prayer for His Readers (1:9-14)

At this point Paul's thanksgiving merges into a noble prayer for his readers. Remembering the dangers that face them from the false teachers, he prays that they may have three things: First, a right knowledge of God's will, which will issue in corresponding moral conduct; second, power to hold joyfully to the course; and third, a spirit of thankfulness for God's redeeming love shown to them in the Fact of Christ. Does any Christian wish to know how to pray for others and what to pray for them? Then let him be guided by these verses. Here are three heavenly boons which any congregation of Christ's people might long to possess: Knowledge of God's will (with conduct to match it), equipment with divine power to run the Christian race, and an ever-thankful spirit for the inestimable love of God to us in Jesus Christ.

But let us study the prayer in more detail.

It may well be that when Paul prays for his readers' growth in "spiritual wisdom" he has in mind the pretentious speculations which some Colossians were mistaking for the true wisdom, the wisdom which, as James says, is "from above" and which "is first pure, then peaceable" and is "full of mercy and good fruits" (James 3:17). Notice, too, how for Paul truth is always "truth in order to goodness." He has no time for a spiritual wisdom which does not issue in "a life worthy of the Lord," that is, of

Christ, and which does not flower in good works. We cannot, however, achieve such a life by our own unaided efforts; only if we are equipped with God's power can we exhibit the "endurance" which is the capacity to see things through, and the "patience" or "long-temperedness" which is the capacity to endure wrongs without retaliating. But, says Paul, to your "endurance and patience" add "joy." So Jesus had counseled his disciples in the last Beatitude (Matt. 5:11-12). The temper called for is no gray and close-lipped Stoicism which can only "grin and bear it," but true Christian serenity which, born in suffering, meets the world with cheerfulness and abounds in thanksgiving.

We shall have frequent occasion in this letter to note how Paul inculcates the Christian duty of thankfulness. The thankfulness called for in verse 12 is not so much that general gratitude for "our creation, preservation, and all the blessings of this life" as the quite specific gratitude to God for his "inestimable love" shown in our redemption. But note Paul's words. "The Father . . . has qualified us to share in the inheritance of the saints in light." No merit of our own has entitled us to this high destiny; it is God who of his grace has "qualified" us—made us fit for it. (For the word and the thought, applied to the Christian ministry, see II Corinthians 3:5-6.) "Inheritance" is more literally "lot," a word often used of the holdings of land which Rome gave her veterans when their fighting days were done. So the King of kings provides for those whose spiritual warfare is accomplished a place "in light," that is, in the presence of him who "dwells in unapproachable light" (I Tim. 6:16).

But salvation, as verse 13 shows, is not merely a future hope; it is also a present blessing. God has already "delivered us from the dominion of darkness and transferred us to the kingdom of his beloved Son." Observe how Paul thinks of man's unregenerate state. He dwells in "the dominion of darkness," a phrase suggesting a realm full of sinister, superhuman forces menacing men's lives, forces which Paul identified with the Devil and his minions. We hardly use this language nowadays; we talk rather of men in the grip of economic forces and at the mercy of inexorable scientific laws. Yet it is far from sure that Paul's language stands for outmoded myth; men have begun again to talk of "the demonic" in our world, as they well might who have seen with their own eyes the depths of deviltry to which great nations can descend and the savage bestiality of men to their fellow men.

But, says Paul, Christians are no longer at the mercy of this dominion of darkness, for God has transferred them (the Greek word is one that is often used of a victorious king *deporting* a conquered people) to "the kingdom of his beloved Son." What is this but the Church over which Jesus reigns as King and Head in all his redeeming grace? "In whom," Paul concludes, "we have redemption, the forgiveness of sins." Does the word "redemption" mystify us? Then, says Paul, it is as simple as this: it means that our sins have been forgiven. The chains which bound us were the spiritual chains of sin and guilt; but God in Christ has struck them off, and we are free. Only those who have never taken sin seriously will count this a boon of no importance. To some men forgiveness may seem an easy thing. The New Testament knows nothing of cheap forgiveness. It insists that just because God is holy, forgiveness must be a very costing thing to him, and it tells us that the price of our forgiveness was the life of God's well-beloved Son.

THE PERSON OF CHRIST AND HIS WORK
Colossians 1:15—2:7

The Cosmic Christ (1:15-20)

This is the most important passage in the letter. Never in all his letters does Paul's thought about Christ soar higher. He gives Christ the freedom of the universe. What impelled Paul to produce this "great Christology," as it has been called?

It was the heresy in Colossae. The heretics, let us recall, by making Christ only one in a series of mediators strung out between the transcendent God and the material world, had scaled down Christ and his work and robbed them of their unique importance. The issue was, and still is, crucial. If Christ is to be truly the Savior of the world, the Christian must be sure not only that Christ is big enough for the task assigned him, but that what he has done is all that is needed for the world's redeeming. Paul is quite sure that, on these counts, Christ more than measures up, as we say; and in this passage he tells his readers that creation actually exists with Christ in view, and that God in Christ has wrought a reconciliation which avails for all created things.

The passage really falls into two parts. In verses 15-17 Paul deals with Christ and creation; in verses 18-20 with Christ and the Church, which is the New Creation. The things he says on each will be set down in summary, then the details of the passage will be considered.

Christ and Creation (1:15-17)

1. Christ is God manifest.
2. In time and dignity he is prior to all creation.
3. In him absolutely everything in the universe has been created, and not only is he God's mediator in creation, but he is creation's goal.
4. It is to him that all things owe their coherence.

Christ and the Church (1:18-20)

1. Christ is the Head of the Church, his Body.
2. As death's first conqueror, he is the sovereign Lord of a great risen host.
3. God in his fullness chose to dwell in him, and through him to reconcile to himself the whole universe.
4. The instrument of this reconciliation is the Cross.

Before the details are treated, it should be remarked that all these stupendous, breath-taking things were being said about Christ only about thirty years after his crucifixion, and that, staggering as they are, they must be said by us, too, if we take seriously our belief in Christ's deity.

Returning to verse 15, we observe first that when Paul calls Christ "the image of the invisible God," he means that he is the visible manifestation of God. When he calls him "the first-born of all creation," he does not mean, as we might infer, that Christ was created before all other created things, as Arius in the Early Church was later to say. The phrase means "One who was in being before creation"; and, since primogeniture generally implied superior dignity, the thought is that Christ is prior in dignity, as well as in time, to all created things.

The "in him" of the next verse (1:16) does not denote agency, but spiritual locality. The creation is an unfolding of the mind of God in Christ. "And," Paul is saying here, "when I say creation, I mean not only the visible world but all those unseen rulers, call them what you will—thrones, dominions, principalities, or powers—whom our heretical friends in Colossae are so keen to include along with Christ in their hierarchy of mediators."

"All things were created through him and for him" (1:16). That means: Christ is not only God's mediator in creation, but also the *goal* to which he is shaping his great purpose in creation. Here is something that Paul has never quite said before. We know from I Corinthians 8:6 that he had conceived of Christ as God's mediator, but now for the first time he says that creation exists with Christ in view, that, in brief, the world was made for Christ.

"He is" (1:17) is probably a declaration of Christ's absolute pre-existence, like the "I am's" of the Fourth Gospel. Christ exists, as God exists, prior in time and in dignity to all things. Paul's last assertion here is that the unity and order of the universe are not accidental; they are due to Christ. The universe owes its coherence to him, and because of him holds together.

Before we turn to consider Christ's relation to the New Creation, we must observe that Paul was enabled so to think of Christ because he equated him with the "divine Wisdom" of the Jewish theologians. In Proverbs 8:22-31 and in the apocryphal Wisdom of Solomon, as well as in other places, there is the concept of a divine Wisdom pre-existent with God and acting as his mediator in creation. Practically everything Paul says about Christ in this passage had been said by the Jewish theologians about this divine Wisdom. What has happened is clear. Casting about for the highest category of thought whereby to set forth the supreme significance of the Savior, Paul found what he wanted in the passages about the divine Wisdom. Jesus Christ, he argues, holds that very place at the heart of ultimate Reality which our theologians once ascribed to Wisdom. We get a hint of the way Paul's mind is moving in I Corinthians 1:24 where he calls Christ "the power of God and the wisdom of God." In Colossians he simply develops and expands the idea. Today, of course, we find it difficult to use this category as Paul did, because it means nothing to our contemporaries. Our task is, using the highest categories and thought-forms familiar to us and our hearers, to give Christ a similarly unique place in the ways of God with men.

In verses 18-20 we pass from Christ the Lord of the universe to Christ the Lord of the Church.

Here Paul's first statement is that Christ "is the head of the body, the church." If you had asked the Apostle whether his description of the Church as Christ's Body was a metaphor or something more, he might have been at a loss for an answer. So are we. Paul certainly sees the Church as a kind of larger incarnation of Christ. Just as once Christ appeared in a body of flesh, so now he dwells in the Church and uses its members to manifest himself to men, and to do his work in the world. We can guess that it was in the context of the early Christian Communion service that this name for the Church was born. There the one loaf, in which all shared, was named Christ's Body (I Cor. 10:16-17). What more natural than that the partakers should come to be called his Body? Perhaps the best illustration of the concept lies in the question of the glorified Christ to Paul the persecutor, "Saul, Saul, why do you persecute me?" (Acts 9:4). If we object that Paul was persecuting Christ's followers, we unwittingly make the point, for we highlight the closeness of the relation between Christ and his followers; to injure his followers is to injure Christ himself. Together, Christ and his people make up one personality, one body. (Had not Jesus himself prepared the way for all this by saying that where two or three were gathered together in his name, there was he in their midst, and by insisting that to befriend one of his helpless brethren was to befriend himself?) In any case, Paul saw the Church as a social organism, indwelt by Christ through the Holy Spirit, and called to continue his work in the world.

Paul had used the doctrine before (in Rom. 12 and I Cor. 12) to show that, while the Church is made up of a great many different people, with widely differing interests and talents, it yet forms one organism—a body wherein all the various members ought to work harmoniously together. But here in Colossians, as in Ephesians, he takes the further step of calling Christ the Body's "Head." Why "head"? Is the primary idea that of *control* (since the head may be said to control the body)? Or is it *supremacy* (since the head may be said to rule the body)? Perhaps the latter is likelier.

Paul's second statement (1:18) is that Christ is "the beginning, the first-born from the dead, that in everything he might be preëminent." We might paraphrase his meaning thus: "Christ is the source of the Church's life, since he rose first from the dead that others might rise through him. Thus in all things (in Church as well as universe) he shows himself supreme."

Thirdly, in explanation of all this (1:19), Paul defines Christ's divine status. "For in him all the fullness of God was pleased to dwell." The Greek word translated "fullness" means "totality," or "plenitude." It was a word the heretics had been bandying about. They thought of the divine nature as made up of a number of powers or "aeons" emanating one from another in descending scale. These powers, taken together, made up, they said, the "totality" of Godhead. Paul takes their word and turns it against them. On the contrary, he says, in Christ "all the fullness of God," that is, the totality of divine powers, chose to make its abode. The phrase claims full deity for Christ. Paul says that "God was in Christ" (II Cor. 5:19) not in some partial way (as might be said of many great human teachers) but in his plenitude.

But "God in his fullness," as we may paraphrase it, not merely chose to dwell in Christ; he willed "through him to reconcile to himself all things, whether on earth or in heaven"; and the instrument of this great purpose of peace was the Cross of Christ, for Paul adds, "making peace by the blood of his cross" (1:20). Here, then, we have not only a cosmic Christ but a cosmic Cross —and the promise of a cosmic peace! Once again we are left marveling at the range and grandeur of Paul's thought: Calvary, the instrument and pledge of God's great design in Christ to end all the tragic disharmonies of the universe and bring everything under one effective rule!

What has Paul told us about Christ in this whole passage? First, that, as God's dear Son, he is his creative Agent and the appointed Goal of the universe; second, that he is the Head of the New Creation, the Church, and the bearer of full deity; and, third, that, through his Cross, he is destined to be God's effective agent of a vast cosmic peace. If we are to be faithful to Paul and the New Testament, some of us will have to think about Christ in bigger terms than we have been accustomed to do.

The Experience of Reconciliation (1:21-23)

Turning from his soaring thoughts about Christ, Paul now appeals to that evangelical experience which should underlie any sound Christian theology. "You know," he says in effect, "what God by Christ has done for you. You who were estranged from his family, God has reconciled to himself. And the deed which procured this blessing was Christ's death in his body of flesh." The phrase "his body of flesh" is so worded as to stress, for the heretics' benefit, the stark reality of Christ's passion. There is no theorizing here about the Atonement; Paul states the fact—and its consequence, the good standing of his readers before God.

Verse 22 describes the first stage in Christian salvation. We have here in essence, if not in the usual language, what Paul means by "justification by faith." Paul does not mean here that at some future time (though some have so interpreted him) those who believe in Christ will become morally perfect in God's sight; he means that here and now, for Christ's sake, God treats them as forgiven people, people who are right with God. Later he will tell them how, by strenuous moral effort, they should *become* what they now potentially *are*—people fit for the presence of the holy God.

But at this point he enters a warning. All this is true provided that they remain "stable and steadfast" in their faith (1:23). They *can* fall away from God's grace if, for example, they allow their heretical brethren in Colossae to undermine their simple trust in the gospel of God's grace. But, of course, not the Colossians only, but all Christians constantly need this warning.

Finally (1:23), as in 1:6, Paul reminds them of the catholicity or universal appeal of the true gospel (see Matt. 28:19). The last word of the verse, "minister," is literally "deacon"; it means, quite simply, one who is in Christ's service, and at that time it had not yet acquired its later technical sense.

The Apostle's Ministry (1:24-29)

Paul's theme has been God's plan for the reconciliation of the world. Now he glances at his own share in it as God's minister. But what does he mean by *completing* "what is lacking in Christ's afflictions for the sake of his body, that is, the church"? He is certainly not thinking of the sufferings which Christ endured on the cross, as though these needed to be supplemented. For Paul, Christ's work on the cross was a finished work. Rather they are the afflictions of the *corporate* Christ. We recall that when Paul persecuted the Christians, he found he was persecuting Christ himself. So close is the union between Christ and his Church that what the Church suffers may be called Christ's sufferings. And so it is here. The afflictions are those which the Church must, in God's providence, undergo till sin is vanquished and God is all in all; and they are the afflictions of Christ because he is the true subject of every experience the Church undergoes in fulfilling God's will. Paul thinks, then, of a sum of sufferings to be made up before the End comes, and he rejoices to play his part in making it up.

Paul does this as a "minister according to the divine office which was given" to him for them (1:25). "Divine office" is a Greek word usually rendered "stewardship." It signifies either the position of an administrator or the exercise of that office, as here. "The commission given me by God" is Paul's meaning. That commission is to make fully known "the word of God" which Paul describes as "the mystery." In the New Testament, a "mystery" does not mean something which must be kept secret except from the initiated. It signifies something which could not be known except by divine revelation but which, though once hidden, is now revealed—"an open secret," as we say. Here the mystery is the divine secret (or purpose), unguessed by past generations but now revealed in Christ—God's plan to offer salvation to the Gentiles through his Messiah, or as Paul puts it, "Christ among you [Gentiles], the hope of glory" (1:27). This we take to be the right interpretation, although some follow the rendering of the Revised Standard Version, "Christ in you," and interpret it mystically on the lines of Paul's "that Christ may dwell in your hearts through faith" (Eph. 3:17).

This is the Savior Paul preaches, his sole aim in his evangelism being "to bring every man as a mature Christian into God's presence," as Paul is saying in substance. Notice the threefold "every man" in verse 28. The devotees of the Greek mystery religions offered their secrets only to the initiated few. By contrast, Paul's gospel is for all men, and to this end he labors with all the energy God gives him. We recall Philippians 2:12-13, where a man's salvation depends on God's work and includes his own efforts. So it is in the work of evangelism.

Verses 25-29 are notable for the light they shed on Paul's conception of his calling as a minister: showing it to be a divine commission (1:25); a proclamation of the gospel—"to make the word of God fully known" (1:25-26); and a cure of souls—to "present every man mature in Christ" (1:28). How does Paul fulfill this calling? With God's help and his own toil (1:29).

Paul and His Readers (2:1-7)

Paul now imagines himself addressing all the Christians in the Lycus Valley. His deep concern is that they should be knit together in love and grow into mature Christians, well able to resist the seductions of the false teachers. "All the riches of assured understanding" (2:2) might be rendered also "all the wealth of conviction that comes from insight" into "God's mystery," Christ. The Revised Standard Version here follows the reading of two of the most ancient Greek manuscripts, and its translation is probably the best; but there are many variants in other manuscripts and versions, of which the likeliest is "the mystery of God, the Father of Christ." Paul adds, "In whom are hid all the treasures of wisdom and knowledge" (2:3). The heretics, who were half Gnostics, apparently prided themselves on their esoteric knowledge. In Christ, Paul replies, we have all the knowledge needed for salvation. But the word "hid" is surprising; we might have expected "revealed." Perhaps Paul means that in Christ we get access to illimitable stores of truth, truth which by its very nature is inaccessible to men except through revelation. "Do not be beguiled by anybody's smooth talking," he is saying in 2:4, warning against persuasive tongues and using a verb which means "lead astray by false reasoning." But he is not unduly worried, for it is as if he were present in the Lycus Valley and, like a general inspecting his troops, can see for himself their "good order" and "firmness." The two Greek words Paul uses here have a military ring, suggesting a well-ordered line of battle with solid depth behind it.

The thing to do, then (2:6-7), is to deepen and confirm their loyalty to Christ as Lord, along the lines already laid down by their missioner Epaphras. "Live in him" means, "Live your life in union with Christ"; for Christianity is much more than merely trying to practice Christ's precepts; it is a day-to-day communion with a living Lord. "Rooted and built up in him" are mixed metaphors to describe a Christian whose whole life is fixed and founded in his Savior. In short, says Paul, be all that Epaphras counseled you to be. Observe how Paul puts complete trust in the teaching of Epaphras, and does not seek to tamper with his colleague's work. It is the part of wisdom in a leader to leave one's lieutenant alone, if he is known to be a good one.

WARNING AGAINST HERETICS
Colossians 2:8-23

The False and the True Doctrine (2:8-15)

Paul now sternly warns his readers against the heretics. "See to it that no one makes a prey of you by philosophy and empty deceit" (2:8). The Greek verb translated "makes a prey of" means literally "kidnap." The heretics are men-stealers! Paul, of course, is not here inveighing against philosophy in general, but against "that humbug masquerading as philosophy" which constituted the Colossian heresy. He describes it as being "according to human tradition," that is, taken over by hearsay from one man to another, and as trafficking in "elemental spirits of the universe." Once interpreters took the Greek word translated here "elements," to mean the ABC, or elementary principles, of religion; but it is now commonly held that, since these "elements" are rivals of Christ, Paul is thinking of "elemental spirits" or angelic beings, supposed to inhabit the stars and control human destinies. The heretics at Colossae, like later Gnostics, seem to have assumed the existence of a whole hierarchy of these beings, strung out as mediators between God and the world. In this hierarchy, it would appear, they gave Christ a place, though perhaps not the highest. Now, for Paul, as for any true Christian, there could be only one mediator, Jesus Christ, and therefore to assign him only a place, however exalted, in a weird hierarchy of this sort was hopelessly to adulterate the Christian faith. So Paul insists here, as Peter is quoted as saying in Acts 4:12, that Christ's is the only "name under heaven" whereby men may be saved. (Does all this talk about "elemental spirits of the universe" sound like so much mumbo-jumbo which no right-thinking twentieth-century man could possibly accept? Then let us remember that some of our newspapers still think it good business to help their readers to cast their horoscopes by supplying them regularly with the necessary astral information. Moreover, it is pertinent to add that one or two of our modern deviationist Christian sects treat Jesus Christ much as did the heretics in Colossae.)

In Christ, Paul insists (2:9-10), "the whole fullness of deity dwells bodily." This statement, which closely resembles that in 1:19, forcibly affirms Christ's divinity. But what precisely does "bodily" signify? The older commentators once took it to mean "incarnately"; but the Incarnation is hardly in Paul's mind here. Others think it means "actually" or "genuinely," that is, in full reality. But the best explanation is "corporately," that is, in one organism or body. So taken, it becomes an apt answer to the heretics. Deity is not distributed up and down a whole series of angelic beings; it is organized in one personality, Christ's. And as the "totality" of Godhead dwells in Christ, so he enables men to reach a full religious experience—"you have come to fullness of life in him." In other words, "You do not need to look elsewhere for a Savior," since Christ is "the head of all rule and authority"—is supreme over every angelic power.

Verses 11-15 form the hardest passage in the whole letter. First (2:11) comes a reference to "circumcision made without hands"—that is, a nonphysical or spiritual one—which Paul's readers have undergone. But surely (someone may say) Paul spent most of the Letter to the Galatians in proving that the Christian has no need for circumcision? Yes, but Paul here is thinking not of the Jewish rite but of its Christian equivalent, baptism. He says that the Colossian Christians "were circumcised . . . by putting off the body of flesh in the circumcision of Christ" (2:11). The allusion in the last phrase is to Christ's own parting with his flesh, his death, which he had called a "baptism." When Christ stripped off his physical body, he was inaugurating that death to self and the old nature in which the Christian is united with him through baptism. For when at baptism a man is joined with Christ, he shares in the virtue of all that Christ did for him by his dying and rising. He dies with Christ to his past and rises with him into newness of life. This, in fact, is what verse 12 says, stating briefly what is said at length in Romans 6:3-11. But baptism is no magical rite, valid in itself, for it depends upon the convert's faith, as Paul now adds—"through faith in the working of God, who raised him from the dead." In Paul's view (as he makes clear in the Romans passage) baptism is valid only if it is a real *moral* death and resurrection for the convert.

Here let us pause to make an important point. We think of baptism mostly as the symbol of *washing*. The New Testament also thinks of it as a *dying and rising*. And naturally so. For New Testament baptism was founded on Christ's own blood-baptism for us—remember his saying, "I have a baptism to be baptized with" (Luke 12:50)—and vividly symbolized the spiritual truth which it conveyed. Recall what normally happened. As Christ had gone down into his baptism of death, so the communicant in the moment of baptism was "buried," as Christ had been in the grave. Then he "rose" into new life, as Christ had risen on the first Easter Day. Nor was all this only bare symbolism. Through the Holy Spirit's working, the convert really rose from his own bad past into a new life; and henceforth he was called to become what he now potentially was—a new man in Christ, united with his living Lord and incorporated into his Body, the Church.

It is of this experience that Paul writes in verse 13. Dead in sin, God gave us new life "with him"—in union with Christ—and forgave us all our trespasses.

The theme of verses 14 and 15 is the Atonement and its efficacy. What Paul says is that Christ by his death has destroyed the Law and has set us free from the tyranny of the evil powers that lie behind the Law. But the wealth of his metaphors makes the passage exasperatingly difficult.

God, Paul says, by Christ's Cross "canceled the bond" which stood against us with its legal demands. "Cancel" is literally "rub out," as one might rub letters off a papyrus. But what is this "bond" with its legal demands which stood against us? The Greek word refers to an IOU, a note signed by the debtor—in this case, ourselves, mankind. All men are under obligation to live by God's Law—his revealed will—with all its demands. But by our sin and wrongdoing we all put ourselves hopelessly into God's debt and have to acknowledge, "We have done the things which we ought not to have done, and have left undone the things which we ought to have done." The *bond* with all its obligations is clearly "against us," approved by our own signature, confessed by our consciences. But this bond Christ, by becoming man, has acknowledged for us, and by his death he has discharged it—blotting out the fatal writing, as Paul's metaphor has it—by accepting the death warrant which the bond constitutes. "This he set aside, nailing it to the cross" (2:14). Some interpreters, though they have no evidence to support them, have said that Paul refers here to the practice of driving a nail through a discharged bond and displaying it in some public place. Possibly, however, the allusion is to the Roman practice of putting a *titulus*, or title, over the cross of a crucified man, briefly setting forth the crime for which he was condemned. If so, instead of "Jesus of Nazareth, the King of the Jews" (John 19:19), Paul imagines another and subtler *titulus* indicating why Christ died: "The Law is canceled by Messiah's death."

To understand the connection of the next verse (2:15) with the one that precedes, let us remember that in late Jewish tradition (which the heretics evidently accepted) the Law was supposed to have been mediated to men by angelic beings, that is, elemental spirits, who, therefore, held men in their baleful power. But now, Paul says, by the Cross of Christ God has not merely canceled the Law with all its damning charges against us, but has triumphed over the angelic beings who stand behind the Law. "He disarmed the principalities and powers [the angelic beings] and made a public example of them, triumphing over them in him." This is another military metaphor. The picture is of Christ as a victorious general doing battle with the supernatural foes of the human race, defeating them, and then despoiling them of their weapons and leading them captive behind his chariot as he enters his capital city in triumph. The metaphor attempts to say something very profound: to see in the Cross a great cosmic victory, won in the unseen world, over the evil forces of the cosmos which bedevil our lives. The Cross is our Lord's death grapple with these powers of evil, a contest through which he comes victorious by the Resurrection. At Calvary a deathblow was dealt to these evil powers, a blow which must in the end prove fatal.

Much in these verses may sound mythological, implying as it does supernatural beings and a conflict among them, all of which the modern man may find difficulty in accepting. But is this way of thinking so very different from our own? Granted that we do not necessarily believe that the warring powers in the universe are personal (many of us, however, have in recent years recovered belief in a personal Devil), do we not still think of ourselves as hemmed in by iron forces and inexorable laws which render all our aspirations futile? In other words, if the forms of our thinking have changed since Paul's day, the basic problem remains the same. And if so, may we not say that through Christ we can reach out, beyond all these menacing forces, to a life of freedom and victory, persuaded that the Power which rules the universe is personal and beneficent, and that, in the Cross and Resurrection of his Son Jesus Christ, he has given us a pledge of his final victory over all evil?

Warning Against Heretical Practices (2:16-23)

Paul now attacks two of the chief errors taught by the heretics. The first was practical (2:16). The heretics not only made much themselves of taboos concerning food and the keeping of holy days, but they were also trying to impose their scruples on the rank and file of the Colossian church. By such taboos and ritual they hoped, presumably, to keep on good terms with the angelic powers. Paul dismisses all this as superficial nonsense, a mere pursuit of shadows, when the reality, Christ, is theirs for the having. Notice that the Judaistic element in the Colossian heresy is strongly in evidence here; for "festival," "new moon," and "sabbath"—that is, annual, monthly, and weekly holy times —all suggest Jewish practices. Note, too, that Sabbathkeeping falls under Paul's strictures. What would he have said of some of our latter-day Sabbatarianism? The comment he makes in verse 17 is the kind of comment the author of Hebrews might have made.

The second error (2:18) was more speculative. The heretics set great store by "self-abasement"—a technical term for fasting —and "worship of angels." "Let no one," Paul is saying to his readers, "disqualify you on this score." "Disqualify" is literally "decide as an umpire against you." Apparently, the heretics were trying to make Epaphras' converts *feel inferior,* because they were naive enough to take Christ alone as their Savior, when they might have had a whole hierarchy of angelic beings to help them!

The phrase translated "taking his stand on visions" has puzzled interpreters. It must describe some pretentious "theosophist" who claims mystical insight on the basis of his visions. The verb Paul uses here appears in an inscription found by Sir William Ramsay, in which the priests of a temple in Asia Minor certify that someone "having received the mysteries" (that is, having undergone preliminary instruction) "entered in." Paul possibly is quoting, half-mockingly, some high-flown phrase used by one of the heretics who claimed to have shared in some mystic observance which revealed final secrets to him.

All people like this, Paul says (2:19), are disloyal to the Head of the Body. They lose effective contact with Christ—"And," he implies, "anybody knows what chance of growth a body has which is severed from its head!" Observe that here "the Head" represents the source of vitality rather than the seat of control. Verse 19 shows Paul employing anatomical terms to describe the Body's functioning—"the whole body, nourished and knit together through its joints and ligaments." If that phrase had occurred in Luke's Gospel or Acts, we should have said at once, "There is Dr. Luke talking professionally." Is it possible that one of his medical friend's phrases lingered in Paul's memory? At any rate, his point is that the heretical tendencies in Colossae were disrupting the Christian fellowship, making it impossible for Christ's Body to grow as God meant it to grow.

At verse 20 Paul harks back to his figure of baptism as a death. By dying with Christ in baptism, his readers had passed right out of the control of these angelic powers. Why then, Paul says, do you persevere in all these petty prohibitions—"Do not handle, Do not taste, Do not touch"—connected with them, since these very human taboos are obviously concerned only with material and perishable things. They may have "an appearance of wisdom in promoting rigor of devotion [self-imposed worship] and self-abasement [fasting] and severity to the body," but for "checking the indulgence of the flesh," they are valueless. (This rendering of the last part of verse 23 in the Revised Standard Version is the best guess at the meaning of some very difficult words. It takes a Greek preposition in its medical sense, in the sense of a remedy *against* some ailment.)

The modern reader may well exclaim again at this point, "What relevance has all this for us? We don't find angel-worshipers in our denomination today." No, but there are still plenty of astrologists and fancy religionists in the world masquerading under Christian colors, as there are still plenty of people who mix up fads about food with their religion. To all Christians who think to read their destiny in the stars, or who think Sabbatarianism or vegetarianism is of the essence of the Faith, Paul can be heard saying, across the centuries, "Christianity is none of these things; it is new life with Christ."

THE NEW LIFE IN CHRIST
Colossians 3:1—4:6

Risen with Christ (3:1-4)

In 2:12 Paul had described baptism as a dying and rising with Christ. The ethical implications of this dying were then discussed in 2:20-23. Now Paul tells his readers what rising with Christ should mean in terms of morals. A passage like this well illustrates his favorite doctrine that the moral conduct of the Christian man is not the *means* by which he earns God's salvation, but the *consequence* of the new relationship to God which he has by faith.

Observe that the mystical rising of Christians with Christ into newness of life (3:1) is regarded as accomplished fact, and not as some future blessing. This is of a piece with the rest of the New Testament's testimony that in the Fact of Christ eternity has invaded time, making salvation a present experience as well as a future hope. So John insists again and again, in Gospel and Epistle, that eternal life, though to be consummated hereafter, is to be had here and now.

Jesus had said, "Where your treasure is, there will your heart be also" (Matt. 6:21). So Paul now says in effect, "Your treasure, Christ, is now enthroned in the heavenly world, and your thoughts and aspirations ought to be there too, with him" (3:1-2). For, as he puts it epigrammatically, "Your life is hid with Christ in God" (3:3). Because Christ is with God, the Christian's destiny, which is bound up with Christ's, is there too. It is a *hidden* destiny. But a time is coming when what is hidden will be revealed. "When Christ who is our life appears, then you also will appear with him in glory" (3:4). This is the event of which the Apostles' Creed speaks: "He shall come . . . " It is the only reference in Colossians to Christ's Second Coming, and Paul pictures it as a making manifest of what is hidden rather than as the catastrophic ending of one age and the spectacular inauguration of another. In other words, the event we call Christ's Coming will be essentially the open unveiling of Christ's Resurrection triumph, and in that unveiling "in glory" those who are Christ's will share.

With "Christ who is our life" we may compare John 14:6: "I am . . . the life"; and with the promise that Christians will appear with Christ in glory, I John 3:2: "Beloved, we are God's children now; it does not yet appear what we shall be, but we know that when he appears we shall be like him, for we shall see him as he is."

Christian Ethics: (1) Off with the Old Habits! (3:5-11)

First, two general observations may be made. (1) Every reader of Paul's letters notices that they fall into two parts, first a doctrinal section, and then an ethical one. The two sections, however, belong together like the two sides of a medal; for Paul's moral imperatives ("Put . . . away" the old habits, and "put on" the new ones) grow out of, and flow from, his doctrinal indicatives ("With Christ you died . . . you have been raised with

Christ"). (2) The argument of this section on Christian ethics
is this: "In principle you have died with Christ to the old life and
risen with him into a new one. Therefore become what you are.
Have you put off the old life? Then really put it off! Have you
put on the new man? Then really put it on." (The metaphors of
putting off and putting on would have special point if at baptism
the convert was made to put off his old clothes and to put on
new ones.) Some may think this pretty poor ethical theory: yet
it goes to the root of the matter. For, as Jesus said, a bad tree
cannot produce good fruit; and unless the seed, or principle, of
goodness is first implanted in a man's life, all the law and exhortation in the world will be useless.

Since you have died with Christ, Paul begins (3:5), you must
"put to death" or kill all use of your faculties for sensual purposes.
He lists a group of five such vices, ending the list, oddly enough,
with "covetousness," which he defines as "idolatry." The Greek
word here means "ruthless and aggressive self-seeking," literally,
the passion to "have more." It can be called idolatry because the
self-seeker makes *gain* his god, and this is just as much idolatry
as bowing down before sticks and stones. If Paul puts the sins of
the flesh in the forefront, as he does here, we must always remember that he was addressing people who had come straight
out of a life where sins of the flesh were rampant. Such sins, he
adds (3:6), incur God's wrath. For a fuller explanation of this
idea we must turn to Romans 1:18-32 where Paul describes,
very powerfully, the divine retribution which has come on the
pagan world for its sins. Nowadays many people revolt from the
very suggestion that God shows wrath. Yet it is basic to Paul's
theology, and, in fact, to any theology which conceives of God
as holy love. It represents a holy God's inevitable reaction to evil
in every shape and form. It is not, as anger so often is with us,
the emotional reaction of an irritated self-concern. We conceive
it best if we imagine the horror a good man feels in the presence
of stark evil, and then multiply by infinity.

Away also, Paul goes on, with all sins of the mind and mouth!
(3:8). And, as before, he lists five of them. How does "anger"
differ from "wrath"? The first is the swift, sudden flame of fury;
the second, the settled disposition. "Malice" is eagerness to harm
one's neighbor. All these, together with lying, should have no
place in people who "have put off the old nature with its practices and have put on the new nature, which is being renewed in

knowledge after the image of its creator" (3:9-10). Paul's thought is that our growing likeness to God (which is sanctification, the work of the Holy Spirit) leads us always onward to the true knowledge of him. "After the image of its creator" recalls Genesis 1:26-27, where man is said to have been created in God's likeness. That image has been defaced by the Fall—that is, by man's sin—but now God designs, in Christ, to restore man to his original status. (Since Christ is earlier called "the image of the invisible God," some would take the phrase here to mean "after the likeness of Christ.")

In this new humanity (3:11) no distinctions of race (like Greek and Jew), or of culture (like Greek and barbarian), or of social standing (like slave and free) count any longer, for "Christ is all, and in all"—that is, he is absolutely everything, everything that matters. ("Scythian," a rude nomad from the northern steppes, typifies the "savage.") A verse like this reveals to us what the true Christian society ought to be. How far we fall short of its ideal in practice, the racial controversies in so-called Christian countries sadly show.

Christian Ethics: (2) On with the New Habits! (3:12-17)

The moral garments of the new life are now suggested in a fivefold list of virtues which, as God's elect and loved people, the Colossians are bidden to assume. "Compassion" and "kindness" describe the Christian temper of mind generally, as "lowliness, meekness, and patience" describe its outgoing to other people. The forgiveness they show one another is to be their response to Christ's own forgiveness of themselves. "On top of all," Paul then says in effect, as though thinking of a belt or sash, "put on love." The followers of the Greek philosopher Pythagoras had once called friendship "the bond of all the virtues"; so Paul thinks of Christian love as the "complete binder" of all the other Christian virtues. In like manner he had called it "the fulfilling [sum total] of the law" (Rom. 13:10) and the greatest of all the Christian's spiritual gifts (I Cor. 13:13).

"The peace of Christ" (3:15) which is to "rule" (the Greek verb means literally "act as umpire") their hearts is the peace which Christ brings (John 14:27), the peace which flows from obedience to him. Such a peace, if it has free course, will compose all conflicts. Paul's words, "to which indeed you were called in the one body," give the theological reason for this: peace is the purpose of their organization in one Body.

Verse 16 can be variously punctuated. The Revised Standard Version adopts a rendering probably as satisfactory as any suggested. By "the word of Christ" Paul means the gospel, the word he *preached* and *was*; it is to "dwell," that is, "make its home" among them richly. And it will do so, as they counsel one another in Christian wisdom and gratefully hymn God's praise in "psalms and hymns and spiritual songs." We must never forget that the Christian Church began as a singing church, and that when it cannot sing, the marks of decay are on it. Some fragments of early Christian hymns have survived in the New Testament. The canticles of Luke 1-2 and the hymnodic chants of praise in Revelation (for example, Rev. 5:9-10, 12-13; 11:17-18; 15:3-4; 19:6-8) leap to mind. Ephesians 5:14 is a stanza of a baptismal hymn, and I Timothy 3:16 sounds like a fragment of an early Christian creed designed to be chanted. It may well be that Philippians 2:6-11 is also an early Christian hymn.

Verse 17 sums up. Whatever they say, whatever they do, they are to say and do "in the name of the Lord Jesus." In the ancient world a name had potency; it stood for the personality; it carried the sense of that person's authority. So we still speak of a magistrate as acting "in the name" of the king or of the law. And therefore, when Paul bids them do all "in the name of the Lord Jesus," he means: "Invoke his help when you act; act with his authority; and let his will be expressed in your action." "Giving thanks to God the Father through him," issues again the summons to Christian thankfulness, with the reminder that Christ is their only true mediator in their approach to God.

The Christian Household (3:18—4:1)

Paul now turns to discuss the Christian family, which is of course the keystone of any Christian society. Let Christ be truly worshiped and served at the family altar, and we need not tremble for the Christian future of any country.

In the "household rules" which follow we have perhaps the earliest example of something that crops up frequently in the rest of the New Testament and in the writings of the Apostolic Fathers. No doubt instructions of this kind were given orally to their converts by the Apostles and their associates. When you are dealing with "babes in Christ" (I Cor. 3:1), simple rules in black and white, like these, are very necessary.

Pagan parallels to such instructions can be found (for example, in Epictetus); and in Judaism we discover similar instructions about how to manage one's family, treat one's son, correct one's children, and the like. The new elements in these Christian directions are (a) the stress upon the *reciprocal* nature of these duties—in other words, Christianity declared that wives, children, and slaves had rights as well as husbands, parents, and masters; and (b) the motive and standard of reference which should inform such relationships, namely, "in the Lord," "in Christ." It is incorporation in the community of Christ which gives a new slant to all conduct.

First of all (3:18-19), Paul discusses the relations that ought to exist between husbands and wives, laying stress on reciprocal duties. "In the Lord" means "in a Christian home." "Care for your wives," Paul says, "and do not be surly to them." This forbidding of surliness in husbands, as of "nagging" by the fathers, shows that the new life in Christ is meant to transform relationships on the everyday level as well as to conquer flagrant vices.

Possibly the case of Onesimus (who was a Colossian) accounts for the fullness of Paul's directions to masters and slaves (3:22—4:1). We must also remember that slaves must have formed a big part of the early Christian community. A slave's obedience should not be that of "eyeservice, as men-pleasers." Conceivably Paul is thinking of superficial work—shall we say, not dusting behind the clock or sweeping under the beds? More probably he has in mind the slave who, as we say, "goes through the motions" without really putting his heart into his work. "Singleness of heart" means, "without ulterior motives." The reward promised the faithful slave (3:24) is "the inheritance," that is, a heavenly destiny. Let those who will, mock this as an "otherworldly" promise. But when most of the greatest men in history have longed for a life higher than this world offers, shall we condemn Paul for encouraging in a slave's heart immortal hopes? In verse 25 Paul is speaking to the slave, not to the master. "The wrongdoer will be paid back for the wrong he has done." A slave might easily suppose that in his very humble station his wrongdoing was of no account. "Dishonesty brings its own nemesis," Paul replies, "for God has no favorites."

In all this we cannot fail to be impressed by Paul's basic principle, which is that the Christian fellowship knows no distinction between slave and free man. Whether bond or free, the Christian man is the slave of his heavenly Lord, as Paul himself was. Now, for the slave, this means that he acquires a full moral personality responsible ultimately to Christ alone. And the effect of this is to make the slave no longer a chattel but a spiritually free agent, whose dignity as a person must never be outraged because he happens to have an inferior social position. This, if it is not a solution of the problem of slavery, is a definitely Christian contribution to a solution.

General Counsels (4:2-6)

First, Paul sounds a summons to spiritual alertness (4:2). "Watch and pray," which is in effect what Paul says, comes to them with the best of all possible guarantees, that of the Lord Jesus (Mark 14:38). Then Paul, almost in parenthesis, introduces the element of intercession, that is, prayer for others. "Give me a place in your prayers," he says, aware what an immense support other people's prayers may be to a man in a tight corner. Yet, observe, he does not bid them pray for his release; he wishes them to ask God to "open to us a door for the word" (4:3). This is one of Paul's favorite figures for an opportunity to preach the gospel (see I Cor. 16:9 and II Cor. 2:12). At the same time, preaching the gospel is often called "declaring the mystery of Christ," especially in Colossians and Ephesians. And doors did open for him, as we know, even in prison. One day his own prison door opened to admit—Onesimus! Paul discussed the gospel with interested Jews who visited him in jail (Acts 28:17, 23-28). And no doubt he commended the gospel to his guards.

Next (4:5) comes advice about how to deal with pagans. "Conduct yourselves wisely toward outsiders" means: "Show tact in your contacts with non-Christians." Since Christian fanatics might easily antagonize pagans, he warns his readers against all graceless and aggressive presentation of the gospel to others. The participial phrase which he adds explanatively—literally, "buying up the (significant) time"—may mean either "making the most of your time" or, perhaps better, "making proper use of the occasion." If the second meaning is right, Paul invites his readers to be alert for chances of personal witness. Seize the chance encounter, the unexpected turn in the conversation, to "say a good word for the Lord Jesus."

The final general counsel (4:6) concerns their speech. "Let your speech always be gracious, seasoned with salt, so that you may know how you ought to answer every one." Shall we call this a culinary metaphor? The picture is of the cook putting in the appropriate pinch of salt to suit the individual palate. But what does "gracious" (literally, "with grace") mean in this context? The word may have something of Paul's characteristic usage; grace, for him, normally means the wonderful kindness of God to sinners. More probably, it retains here its old classical sense of "charm" or "attractiveness." Similarly, the classical phrase "Attic salt," that is, "wit," probably explains what is meant by "seasoned with salt." "Let your speech (with outsiders) have charm and wit." There is no benediction on those who present the gospel insipidly; nor does God mean any Christian to be a sanctimonious bore. We are called in our contacts with non-Christians to use all the attractiveness we can command. And, in fact, most of God's persuasive evangelists, from John Chrysostom to Henry Drummond, have been living examples of Paul's precept.

GREETINGS AND BLESSINGS
Colossians 4:7-18

Tychicus and Onesimus (4:7-9)

The section from 4:7 to the end of the letter might be entitled "The Church in Paul's House." The letter draws to its close with personal matters. Paul does not need to go into details because Tychicus and Onesimus, who are traveling together to the Lycus Valley, will tell them all. Tychicus was a friend of Paul's, a native of Asia (probably Ephesus), whom he had included among the Gentile representatives who accompanied him on his last visit to Jerusalem (Acts 20:4). Paul calls him a "faithful minister"—the Greek word being "deacon," that is, anyone engaged in the service of Christ—and a "fellow servant in the Lord," that is, partner in that voluntary bondage to Christ which is Paul's proudest privilege. "I have sent" represents a Greek tense which should be rendered by an English present, "I am sending." Note Paul's fine courtesy in specially commending the runaway Colossian slave, Onesimus, who is the central figure in Paul's Letter to Philemon. But he neither calls him a slave nor alludes to his past history. No, he is "the faithful and beloved brother, who is one of yourselves" (4:9). This selfsame slave probably lived to become Bishop of Ephesus; but this is another story, to be told in the proper place.

Closing Salutations (4:10-18)

First (4:10-11), three Jewish Christians send their greetings. From Acts 19:29 and 20:4 we know that "Aristarchus" was a Thessalonian, that he shared Paul's dangers in Ephesus, and that he had been one of the delegation Paul took up to Jerusalem on his final visit there. Later still (Acts 27:2), he was Paul's companion on the voyage to Rome. "My fellow prisoner" may mean that he shared Paul's Roman prison. More probably, like "fellow servant" (4:7), it means "fellow captive" of the conquering Christ (see II Cor. 2:14).

"Mark"—John Mark, the cousin of Barnabas—is the writer of the Second Gospel. The estrangement between Paul and Mark caused by Mark's desertion at Perga (Acts 13:13 and 15:38) is obviously a thing of the past. Paul hints that Mark may shortly be visiting the Lycus Valley.

"Jesus who is called Justus" possessed two names, like Paul and Mark: one his Jewish name, the other a Greek one, for use in the Gentile world. Nothing further is known of him.

Verse 11 has a certain pathos. Paul is saying in effect, "These are the only friendly Jewish Christians with me, but what a tonic they have proved." The word translated "comfort" possibly has the medical meaning of "tonic." Most Jewish Christians apparently cold-shouldered Paul, and he felt it deeply. Incidentally, this verse, which clearly distinguishes three Jewish Christians in Paul's company from three Gentile ones, is the main evidence that Luke was a Gentile.

Next (4:12-14) three Gentile Christians add their greetings: "Epaphras" is mentioned also in 1:7, a Colossian who had probably founded the churches in the Lycus Valley. Laodicea and Hierapolis, about ten miles south of Colossae, were commercial cities of much importance beside the Lycus River. Poor Epaphras had worried greatly about the heresy which was spreading in his congregations, and had "agonized" about it in his prayers. (The translation "remembering you earnestly in his prayers" is hardly strong enough.)

"Luke the beloved physician" (4:14) is, of course, also the

author of the Third Gospel, and of the Acts of the Apostles (see Philemon 24 and II Tim. 4:11). It is worth noting that the writers of both the Second and Third Gospels were with Paul at this time, which disproves the contention of those who say that Paul knew next to nothing about the historical Jesus.

"Demas" is also mentioned in Philemon 24. In II Timothy 4:10 Paul says, "Demas, in love with this present world, has deserted me." We may conjecture that, having been Paul's associate, he had gone back to worldly business.

And now (4:15) Paul sends his own greetings to the Christians in Laodicea "and to Nympha and the church in her house." We remember Lydia and her house church in Philippi (Acts 16:15). At this time there were no Christian churches of stone and mortar. Probably a room in a house was set apart as a church. Not so long ago some American archaeologists uncovered a house at Dura-Europos on the Euphrates, in which one of the rooms had been so set apart.

When the Colossians have read this letter (4:16), they are to send it to the neighboring church at Laodicea and ask in return for a reading of the "letter from Laodicea." This is probably one of Paul's lost epistles, not the Letter to the Ephesians. The verse warns us against supposing that Paul threw off his letters casually, with no thought whatever of their being read by people beyond the congregation addressed. The fact is that they bore the character of addresses rather than of letters, and that Paul expected them to have a wider circulation. Possibly he foresaw, too, that the people who received them would have them copied and preserved. In this way the body of Pauline literature gradually took shape.

"And say to Archippus, 'See that you fulfil the ministry which you have received in the Lord ' " (4:17). See Philemon 2, where he is called Paul's "fellow soldier." It is a plausible guess that Archippus had been acting as temporary supply in the Lycus Valley churches while their pastor Epaphras was absent in Rome, and it almost sounds as if he had not been concentrating on his work.

Up to this point (4:18) Paul has dictated his letter to a scribe (see Rom. 16:22). Now he adds a greeting in his own hand, as in Galatians 6:11 and II Thessalonians 3:17. It is very touching in its brevity. But his injunction, "Remember my fetters," is a summons to fidelity as well as a pathetic invitation. The letter ends with a prayer for "grace."